MARY TODD LINCOLN

Other titles in *Historical American Biographies*

Alexander Graham Bell
Inventor and Teacher
ISBN 0-7660-1096-1

Andrew Carnegie
Steel King and
Friend to Libraries
ISBN 0-7660-1212-3

Annie Oakley
Legendary Sharpshooter
ISBN 0-7660-1012-0

Benjamin Franklin
Founding Father and Inventor
ISBN 0-89490-784-0

Billy the Kid
Outlaw of the Wild West
ISBN 0-7660-1091-0

Buffalo Bill Cody
Western Legend
ISBN 0-7660-1015-5

Clara Barton
Civil War Nurse
ISBN 0-89490-778-6

Daniel Boone
Frontier Legend
ISBN 0-7660-1256-5

Dolley Madison
Courageous First Lady
ISBN 0-7660-1092-9

George Armstrong Custer
Civil War General and
Western Legend
ISBN 0-7660-1255-7

Jane Addams
Nobel Prize Winner and Founder
of Hull House
ISBN 0-7660-1094-5

Jeb Stuart
Confederate Cavalry General
ISBN 0-7660-1013-9

Jefferson Davis
President of the Confederacy
ISBN 0-7660-1064-3

Jesse James
Legendary Outlaw
ISBN 0-7660-1055-4

Jim Bowie
Hero of the Alamo
ISBN 0-7660-1253-0

John Wesley Powell
Explorer of the Grand Canyon
ISBN 0-89490-783-2

Lewis and Clark
Explorers of the Northwest
ISBN 0-7660-1016-3

Mark Twain
Legendary Writer and Humorist
ISBN 0-7660-1093-7

Martha Washington
First Lady
ISBN 0-7660-1017-1

Mary Todd Lincoln
Tragic First Lady
of the Civil War
ISBN 0-7660-1252-2

Paul Revere
Rider for the Revolution
ISBN 0-89490-779-4

Robert E. Lee
Southern Hero of the
Civil War
ISBN 0-89490-782-4

Robert Fulton
Inventor and
Steamboat Builder
ISBN 0-7660-1141-0

Stonewall Jackson
Confederate General
ISBN 0-89490-781-6

Susan B. Anthony
Voice for Women's Voting Rights
ISBN 0-89490-780-8

Thomas Alva Edison
Inventor
ISBN 0-7660-1014-7

Historical American Biographies

MARY TODD LINCOLN

Tragic First Lady of the Civil War

Mary E. Hull

Enslow Publishers, Inc.

40 Industrial Road   PO Box 38
Box 398   Aldershot
Berkeley Heights, NJ 07922   Hants GU12 6BP
USA   UK
http://www.enslow.com

Library of Congress Cataloging-in-Publication Data

Hull, Mary E.
    Mary Todd Lincoln : tragic first lady of the Civil War / Mary E. Hull.
      p. cm. — (Historical American biographies)
    Includes bibliographical references (p.) and index.
    Summary: A biography of the wife of the sixteenth president of the
United States, discussing her upbringing, marriage, her role in Lincoln's
political career, and the tragedies that marred her life.
    ISBN-10: 0-7660-1252-2
      1. Lincoln, Mary Todd, 1818–1882 Juvenile literature. 2. Presidents'
spouses—United States—Biography Juvenile literature. [1. Lincoln, Mary
Todd, 1818–1882. 2. First ladies. 3. Women Biography.] I. Title.
II. Series.
E457.25.L55H85 2000
973.7'092—dc21
   [B]   99-20080
                                             CIP
ISBN-13: 978-0-7660-1252-3

Printed in the United States of America

10 9 8 7 6

To Our Readers:
We have done our best to make sure all Internet addresses in this book were
active and appropriate when we went to press. However, the author and the
publisher have no control over and assume no liability for the material available
on those Internet sites or on other Web sites they may link to. Any comments or
suggestions can be sent by e-mail to comments@enslow.com or to the address on
the back cover.

Illustration Credits: Enslow Publishers, Inc., pp. 61, 69; Francis
Browne, *The Everyday Life of Abraham Lincoln* (Hartford: Park
Publishing Co., 1886), pp. 49, 53; Library of Congress, pp. 24, 29, 45,
71, 89, 94; National Archives, pp. 6, 74, 75, 82, 91, 95, 98; Reproduced
from the *Dictionary of American Portraits*, Published by Dover
Publications, Inc., in 1967, pp. 12, 65, 85, 101, 103, 110, 117.

Cover Illustration: Corel Corporation (Background—The White
House); National Archives (Inset).

CONTENTS

Mary Todd Lincoln

1

A CONTROVERSIAL WOMAN

As the Civil War raged between the states in 1863, Mary Todd Lincoln endured a painful personal trial of her own. The charming First Lady with the Kentucky drawl was labeled a traitor to the Union by gossips and reporters who suspected she was sympathetic to the Southern cause. Critics accused Mary Todd Lincoln of betraying her country because she came from a large Kentucky family that, in part, supported the Confederacy. In fact, one of Mary Todd's Confederate relatives had visited her at the White House, much to the astonishment of some Northerners.

In 1863, Mary Todd Lincoln's younger half sister, Martha Todd White, the wife of a Confederate officer, wrote to President Abraham Lincoln, requesting a pass that would allow her to cross enemy lines and come to Washington, D.C. White explained that she needed to purchase some items of clothing for herself that were not available due to blockades in the South. Though Mary Todd and White were from the same Kentucky family, circumstances caused them to lead very different lives. Mary Todd had married Abraham Lincoln, who later became the president of the United States. White had married a man from Alabama and moved to Selma, where she supported the Confederacy. When he received White's letter, President Lincoln reluctantly sent his sister-in-law a pass. Mary Todd felt obligated to do something for her sister, but the two women, born eighteen years apart, barely knew each other. Pass in hand, White traveled past the Union Army to Washington, D.C., with a pile of trunks.

While in the Union capital, White called on the Lincolns at the White House, but perhaps not wanting to condone her behavior, they refused to see her. Martha Todd White stayed in a nearby hotel instead, where she proceeded to embarrass the Lincolns by demonstrating in favor of the Confederacy. Mary Todd Lincoln had already been hurt by reports in the press that claimed she harbored Confederate sympathies. Now her half sister's visit made things much worse for her. According to Todd family history,

Martha Todd White left Washington with her trunks full of quinine, a valuable medicine desperately needed by the Confederate Army.[1] Although this rumor was never proven, it was widely believed, and it had a devastating effect on Mary Todd Lincoln. Critics said she had helped her half sister secure contraband articles to aid the South. Mary Todd Lincoln was accused of being a traitor to the Union, and there were rumors that she had given military secrets to White.

The charges against Mary Todd Lincoln were serious enough that the Congressional Joint Committee on the Conduct of War convened to discuss them. The committee was stopped when President Lincoln appeared before it to solemnly announce that neither he nor his wife harbored Confederate sympathies or had passed any compromising information to the enemy. Though the accusations that Mary Todd Lincoln was a Confederate spy were untrue, she was forever tainted by suspicion.

A Family Divided

Like many other families from states that bordered both the North and the South, the Todd family of Kentucky was divided during the Civil War. Some of the Todds joined the Confederacy and participated in the fight to preserve states' rights, slavery, and the Southern way of life. Of Mary Todd's thirteen siblings, eight supported the Confederacy. Three of her brothers died defending the South. But Mary Todd's five other brothers and sisters, like her, had sided with the Union. When Mary Todd's husband, whom friends of the Todds criticized for his sympathetic attitude toward African Americans, became president of a divided United States in 1861, she had to endure criticism from her own family. Though she supported her husband's politics, Mary Todd was placed in the position of trying to explain his views to her proslavery Kentucky relatives.

Mary Todd Lincoln's family relationships were strained, and in some cases, broken forever. Emilie Todd, Mary Todd's beloved half sister, married a promising young West Point graduate from Kentucky named Ben Hardin Helm. Both Mary Todd and Abraham Lincoln were close to the Helms. When the Civil War began, Lincoln offered his brother-in-law Ben Helm a high position in the Union Army. However, Helm was unable to side against his native South, and in a move that utterly devastated the Lincolns, he joined the Confederate Army. In 1863, Helm was killed at the Battle of Chickamauga.

Widowed, his wife, Emilie, tried to make her way back to Kentucky. She was detained by Union forces who insisted that she swear allegiance to the United States before entering Union territory. Defending her husband's honor, Emilie Todd Helm refused. The soldiers, who knew she was Mary Todd

Lincoln's sister, sent her to Washington, where she and Mary Todd had a tearful reunion. They did not speak about the war. It was too painful for them to discuss.

Despite their different loyalties, however, Emilie Todd Helm and Mary Todd Lincoln still loved each other. The Lincolns welcomed Emilie Todd, and she stayed with them for a week. The presence of a Confederate widow in the White House raised the eyebrows of many Northern politicians, who questioned the Lincolns' propriety. But Mary Todd and Abraham Lincoln were simply experiencing what

A Rebel in the White House

New York Senator Ira Harris, on meeting Mary Todd Lincoln and her half sister Emilie Todd Helm in the White House, asked Mary Todd why her son Robert, then age twenty, had not yet joined the army. "I have only one son," the senator reminded Mary Todd Lincoln, "and he is fighting for his country." Then Senator Harris said to Emilie, who was a Confederate widow, "[I]f I had twenty sons they should all be fighting the rebels." She quickly replied, "And if I had twenty sons they should all be opposing yours." Though the senator complained that the president should not be housing a Confederate in the United States executive mansion, Lincoln politely informed him that "my wife and I are in the habit of choosing our own guests."[2]

As the president leading the United States through the Civil War, Abraham Lincoln also faced personal problems, including conflicts over the war among his family and in-laws.

many families felt during the war as they found themselves on different sides of a Northern-Southern argument that could not always extinguish family love.

In the end, though, Mary Todd's relationship with Emilie Todd Helm did not survive. Upon her return to Kentucky, Emilie tried to use her connections with the president to secure a license to sell cotton. Lincoln was unable to grant her request while Emilie remained a Confederate, but she refused to switch her allegiance. Instead, she lashed out at Mary Todd, blaming her and President Lincoln for the deaths of her husband and their brothers. Unable to forgive Emilie, Mary Todd never spoke to her half sister again.

A Lonely Woman

Mary Todd Lincoln broke off relationships with many of her friends and family members during the course of her life. Unable to forgive them for what she considered a terrible breach of friendship, Mary Todd carried on without them. Sometimes it was a divided family opinion on the Civil War that caused the breach, and sometimes it was because a friend betrayed her with an accusation about her conduct as First Lady. Later in her life, there were those who failed to speak out in her defense, including her own son, when she faced enormous adversity. Though she was one of fourteen Todd children and made many friends during her lifetime, Mary Todd was

often lonely. After the assassination of her husband and the deaths of three of her four sons, she was practically friendless. Mary Todd Lincoln had changed from a cheerful, enterprising woman to a suffering, lonely person accused of treachery, greed, and insanity. As a result, she was robbed of her place as one of the most important and influential First Ladies in the history of the United States.

2

GIRLHOOD IN LEXINGTON, KENTUCKY

Mary Ann Todd was born in Lexington, Kentucky, on Sunday, December 13, 1818, to Eliza and Robert Todd, who were members of Lexington's most prominent families. They lived in a two-story brick house in the center of town. By the time Mary Ann Todd was born, Lexington was one of the most cosmopolitan towns in the American West.

Mary's grandfathers, Robert Parker and Levi Todd, were early pioneers who had helped settle Lexington in the summer of 1775, arriving there on the wilderness road marked by frontiersman Daniel Boone that same year. They built forts to protect themselves from the Choctaw and Catawba Indians, who resented the settlement of whites on what had been their tribal lands. Robert Parker and Levi Todd named the town Lexington after the Battle of Lexington that had opened the Revolutionary War. After the war, Lexington was advertised as a good place for patriots to live, and the population began to grow. The 1790 census showed there were more than one hundred thousand settlers living west of the Appalachian Mountains in what would become the states of Kentucky and Tennessee.[1] By 1820, there were 5,279 people living in Lexington, roughly one third of them slaves.[2] The Todds and Parkers intermarried extensively, creating the first family dynasty in Lexington.

Life in the Todd Household

Mary was the third child born into a family that already included her older sisters, Elizabeth and Frances. A year later, in 1819, her younger brother Levi was born. The following year, another brother, Robert Parker Todd, arrived. The five Todd children lived with their parents and at least three female slaves, who helped Eliza Todd with the cleaning, laundry, cooking, and child care. Although the slaves actually belonged to Mary's grandmother, a wealthy widow, they were on loan to Eliza and Robert Todd to help the family with domestic chores. Mary's father was a slaveholder, but he was against the selling of slaves. He also supported the Kentucky Colonization Society, an organization that raised money to send freed slaves back to Africa.

Mary Ann Todd

When Mary Ann Todd was five years old, her mother had another baby girl, whom she named Ann Todd, after her sister. From this time on, Mary Ann's double name was shortened to just Mary. Mary resented giving up her name and her place as the baby to her younger sister.

Some of the Todds were proslavery and others were antislavery. From the time she was a little girl, Mary Todd was aware of the debate slavery provoked. Mary and her siblings knew, for example, that Mammy, the Todds' chief female slave, had marked the fence behind their house with a sign indicating that it was a safe house where escaped slaves could seek food or brief rest at night. All the Todd children knew this, but their parents probably did not.

In 1825, when Mary was just six years old, her mother, Eliza, died from complications associated with childbirth. Mary had gained a new brother, George Todd, but she had lost her mother. Like many other children growing up in the nineteenth century, Mary Todd learned about death at an early age. Her younger brother Robert had died at fourteen months from a bacterial infection, and now her mother was gone, too. Her mother's death left Mary feeling anxious and sorrowful.[3]

Just six months after her mother's death, Mary's father proposed to a woman named Elizabeth, or "Betsey," Humphreys. Mary's father was anxious to remarry because he needed a mother to take care of his children and his home. But Mary, along with her brothers and sisters, did not like their new stepmother. More than the other children, Mary did not get along with Betsey Todd. Betsey Todd soon began to have her own children—a total of nine in all—and soon the house was filled with the five original Todd children and their half brothers and half sisters.

Of all her relatives, Mary Todd's favorite was Grandmother Parker, who showed Mary special attention. Mary enjoyed this attention because she was the odd girl out in the family. Her older sisters, Elizabeth and Frances, were very close, and her younger sister, Ann, was the favorite of their aunt Ann. The boys were close to their father. Mary felt closest to Grandmother Parker, who sometimes gave her little presents or money for clothes.

From the time she was a little girl, Mary was interested in fashion. When she was nine, she became fascinated by the hoopskirts that were the fashion among the women of Lexington. But Mary's stepmother thought that a nine-year-old was too young to wear a hoop. One day, Mary ingeniously devised two hoops by weaving willow reeds into a circle and appeared before her stepmother wearing her white cotton dress stretched tightly over the homemade hoops. When her stepmother told her to take the hoops off, Mary burst into tears. Her stepmother repeated the story so often, it became a family joke. Mary, who felt humiliated by it, always hated the story.

Eventually, Mary got even with her stepmother by putting salt in her coffee, which caused Betsey Todd to call her "a limb of Satan loping down the broad road leading to destruction."[4] Betsey Todd often tried to shame the Todd children into behaving by referring to them as a "limb of Satan." But she

Lexington Ladies
Mary Todd Lincoln came by her love of high fashion naturally. The women of her birthplace, Lexington, Kentucky, were known for wearing thin satin slippers and for putting on lots of rouge and sporting formal dresses as daywear. One transplanted New Englander, Mary Holley, was shocked by this custom. She wrote that she "was astonished to see callers arrive [before noon] in satin and silk as if they were going to an evening function. No Boston lady would ever be so conspicuous. 'How is Dr. Holley,' they would ask and would adjust their flounces, scarcely touching their backs to the parlor chair lest they form a wrinkle or disturb a hair."[5]

called them "limbs of Satan" so often, the children used the term to make fun of her.

With a house full of children, the Todds were eager to send some of them off to school. The Todd family also believed in the education of girls, even though most girls in Lexington did not attend school. Both Mary's mother and stepmother had gone to school, and her father decided that Mary was going to get an education, too. Among other things, he considered an education a means of making a woman interesting and attractive to potential suitors. When Mary was nine, her father enrolled her in Shelby Female Academy, also known as the Ward Academy, in Lexington. Mary was a student for the next ten years. Only a few thousand American women at this time had more than four years of formal education. Mary Todd was a very well-educated woman for her time.

Mary and Elizabeth Humphreys, a niece of Betsey Todd's, walked to school early each morning, and came home for lunch. School ran from September to January and then from March to July. Mary was taught reading, writing, grammar, math, history, geography, natural science, religion, and French. Her father paid extra in order for her to have French lessons.

Mary Todd Takes to Politics

Mary grew up listening to her father—a businessman, Lexington councilman, and candidate for the state legislature—discuss politics. She was interested in politics much more than other children her age. Politics was not considered a proper topic of conversation for ladies, and Mary's enthusiasm for political issues as a young girl was unusual. Mary sided with the Whigs, her father's political party. At age nine she refused to see Democratic candidate Andrew Jackson when he appeared in Lexington before the presidential election of 1828. A celebration was held in his honor, but Mary boycotted it. As a young girl, Mary argued about Jackson's potential as a presidential candidate with a pro-Jackson neighbor. Her interest in politics caught her father's attention. In fact, Mary may have pursued her interest in politics partly because it made her busy father pay attention to her.

In 1832, at age fourteen, Mary Todd enrolled in a Lexington boarding school known as Mentelle's for Young Ladies, run by Charlotte and Augustus Mentelle. Most girls her age would be finished with their formal education by that age, but Mary was going on for more schooling. Because her stepmother had so many children at home, she probably preferred to have Mary stay in school. Mary became a five-day boarder at Mentelle's, returning home only on weekends, even though the Todd home was less than two miles away. This arrangement was unusual. Students who lived close to school usually did not board. Mary probably boarded during the week because the Todd house was full and because she and her stepmother did not get along.

The Mentelles were French aristocrats who had fled France after the French Revolution, a time when many wealthy Parisians were being killed by democratic revolutionaries because they were members of the upper class. Charlotte Mentelle, the school mistress, often spoke of the French royalty, in whom Mary developed an interest. Mary perfected her French, participated in theater, and starred in several school productions at Mentelle's. Lonely after her mother's death, Mary finally felt she had found her "true" home at Mentelle's.[6]

The Todds Survive a Cholera Epidemic

While Mary was making her home at Mentelle's, her father moved the Todd family to a new home on Main Street in Lexington. With five children from his first marriage and an eventual nine from his marriage to Betsey Todd, Robert Todd needed a larger house. The new home was also a grander place. There, the Todds kept one slave for each white member of the household.

Mary was visiting her family in this new house one weekend in the summer of 1833, when a cholera epidemic broke out in Lexington. Because heavy rains had caused sewage to run into the river, the town's water supply had been contaminated with cholera bacteria. People were infected by the bacteria when they drank or bathed in the river water or ate uncooked foods that had been washed in the water. Those who contracted cholera experienced stomach cramps, diarrhea, vomiting, dehydration, and often death. More than five hundred of the town's seven thousand residents died during the epidemic, which lasted nearly a month.

Because she was home from school for the weekend when the outbreak occurred, Mary, along with the other Todd children, was quarantined, or shut up, in the new Todd house on Main Street. Quarantines were thought to be a way of preventing the spread of disease. People stayed in their homes, going outdoors only when absolutely necessary. For three weeks, the Todds stayed indoors. Because no one went out, they nearly ran out of food before the epidemic was over. So many people died from cholera in such a short time in Lexington that the town ran out of coffins and places to bury people. The town had to start a new cemetery. To help out, Mary's father had all the trunks and boxes in their attic emptied so they could be donated to use as coffins. All the Todds, as well as their slaves, managed to avoid getting cholera. But when Mary returned to Mentelle's school after the outbreak was over, many of her school friends were gone.

Gradually, the shock of the epidemic passed and the town resumed its normal activities. As a young woman in her early teens, Mary began to participate more in the town's social scene. Mary's older sisters,

This is one of the earliest known photographs of Mary Todd.

Elizabeth and Frances, had already entered Lexington society with its busy calendar of dances, dinners, and parties. With slaves to do most domestic tasks, unmarried white women from well-to-do families had little to do except attend social functions, where they were eventually supposed to find a husband. Mary learned to waltz and to do group dances like the quadrille, a kind of square dance. Always at ease making conversation, Mary had no trouble speaking at social events. She was good at mimicking others and sometimes did so at their expense. Mary Todd was known for being quick-witted and having a sharp tongue. Adamant about politics, she sometimes made remarks that offended people of different political persuasions.

Despite her family's prominent social position and her own reputation for being lively and an engaging conversationalist, Mary Todd felt alone during her teens. She described this period of her life as a time "when friends were few."[7]

The original Todd children did not feel at home in the family's new house in Lexington. This was not their mother's house. Here, their stepmother, Betsey Todd, presided. Mary's younger brother George Todd admitted in later life that their stepmother preferred her own children to them, leaving the first Todds no choice but to leave home as soon as they could. Living in such uncomfortable conditions, all the Todd girls took their first opportunity to leave.

Mary Todd preferred life at boarding school to living at home. Her oldest sister, Elizabeth, found her escape through marriage. At age nineteen, she married Ninian Edwards, the son of the Illinois governor, and moved to Springfield, Illinois. Soon afterward, Mary's other older sister, Frances, left Lexington to live at Elizabeth's home in Springfield.

Mary Visits Springfield

In 1836, when she was eighteen, Mary finished her fourth and final year at Mentelle's. She wanted to follow her sisters to Springfield but had to wait until the spring of 1837 before she could make the journey. Without good roads, traveling was difficult. The trip from Lexington to Springfield, which takes only hours by car today, then took two weeks. Spring was really the only good time to attempt the journey. In the summer, the roads were dusty and the riverbeds were muddy and hard to cross. Winter was more treacherous, because the snow on the Illinois prairie could be fierce. A few years earlier, in 1831, more than twenty people had frozen to death trying to cross the prairie in winter.

Mary Todd had to have a traveling partner, too. It was not proper for a woman to travel alone. Traveling women were usually accompanied by a male companion. An unmarried woman could be escorted by a male relative, such as a father, brother, or cousin. Mary Todd's father probably traveled with her on the first leg of her journey in the spring of 1837, the train trip from Lexington to Frankfort, Kentucky. From there, Mary Todd rode a stagecoach to Louisville, where she was picked up by a Springfield relative for the remainder of the journey. Mary Todd had an uncle living in Springfield as well as a cousin, John Todd Stuart, a young lawyer who shared a practice in town with a man named Abraham Lincoln. Most likely, either John Todd Stuart or her uncle met Mary Todd in Louisville and accompanied her up the Mississippi River to Alton, Illinois, by steamboat. From there, they would have taken another stagecoach ride one hundred miles east to Springfield.

After two weeks of traveling, roadside hotels, and bumpy stagecoach rides, Mary Todd finally arrived at her sister Elizabeth Todd Edwards's home. Elizabeth and her husband, Ninian Edwards, lived in a fashionable section of Springfield, which was then a growing town of two thousand people. Their home was large, and it comfortably housed the Edwardses, their baby, Mary's sister Frances Todd, and through the summer of 1837, Mary. Mary Todd made new friends in Springfield. Living next door to the Edwardses was Mercy Levering, an unmarried woman near Mary's age with whom Mary Todd became close. Mary Todd enjoyed the social gatherings that often took place at her sister's house, including the parlor talk of politics, and whether John Todd Stuart or Ninian Edwards would run for

Congress. Her quick tongue and wit enlivened these gatherings. Ninian Edwards said of her, "Mary could make a bishop forget his prayers."[8]

While Mary Todd was first visiting Springfield, another of the town's newest residents, Abraham Lincoln, was beginning his law practice with John Todd Stuart. Twenty-eight years old, Abraham Lincoln was the son of a backwoods farmer. He had met Stuart while he was a militia captain in the war fought by the Americans against the Black Hawk Indians to push the Indian tribe farther westward, to make room for white settlement. Stuart had encouraged Lincoln to study law, and Lincoln had done so in New Salem, Illinois. One contemporary described the young Lincoln as "a raw, tall very countrified looking man yet who spoke with such force and vigor that he held the close attention of all."[9] By 1837, Lincoln had been elected to the Illinois legislature and moved to Springfield to begin work as a junior law partner with John Todd Stuart. Uncomfortable in social situations, Lincoln did not enjoy Springfield as Mary Todd did. "This thing of living in Springfield is rather a dull business, after all; at least it is so to me," he wrote,

> I am quite as lonesome here as ever was anywhere in my life. I have been spoken to by but one woman since I've been here, and should not have been by her if she could have avoided it. I've never been to church yet, nor probably shall not be soon. I stay away because . . . I should not know how to behave myself.[10]

This early photograph of Abraham Lincoln shows the tall, lanky frontier lawyer as he began to break into politics.

Mary Todd thoroughly enjoyed herself in Springfield, but she eventually had to return to Lexington. She did not want to go, but the financial depression of 1837 had hurt Ninian Edwards's business interests, and he could not even afford to pay his taxes. It was expensive for the Edwardses to host an additional guest in their home. Robert Todd had given his daughter Frances Todd money to cover her room and board at the Edwardses', but he had not given Mary Todd any money. Embarrassed by Mary's flight to Springfield, he wanted her to stay with the family in Lexington.[11] Without any money of her own, Mary Todd was left with no choice but to take the long journey back to Kentucky in the fall of 1837.

As soon as she returned to Lexington, Mary Todd began working as an apprentice teacher at the first school she had attended, the Ward Academy. She helped Sarah Ward with the younger children. Certainly Mary Todd did not have to work. She could have lived at her father's home and done nothing but attend parties. Biographer Jean H. Baker believed that Mary Todd may have wanted to become a schoolteacher so that she could afford to return to Springfield on her own. This makes sense, because Mary Todd's female role models, Sarah Ward and Charlotte Mentelle, were both school-teachers, and teaching school was the only way for a woman of her background to properly earn a living.

But in the spring of 1839, another opportunity for Mary Todd to return to Springfield arose when Frances Todd married a doctor and moved out of her sister's home in Springfield. Eager to leave Lexington, twenty-year-old Mary Todd once again undertook the long trip to Springfield and moved back in with the Edwardses.

3

THE BELLE OF SPRINGFIELD

Mary Todd returned to the Edwardses' Springfield home in the spring of 1839 with enthusiasm. She was reunited with her friend and neighbor Mercy Levering, and the two young ladies attended events and parties in town together. As a state legislator, Ninian Edwards was always entertaining guests, and Mary Todd's sister Elizabeth frequently played hostess. The Edwardses' home was an exciting place to live, and one that exposed Mary Todd to all of the eligible young men in town. Among her male admirers were Stephen Douglas and Edwin Webb, both aspiring politicians.

A typical day for Mary Todd began with her morning ritual of writing letters to friends and

relatives. It was customary for ladies to exchange letters frequently, and Mary Todd, like many other women, used letter writing as a means of expressing her emotions. After her friend Mercy Levering married and moved away, for example, Mary Todd continued to confide in her through letters, writing about her Springfield beaus. In her letters, she said things she would not have dared to say out loud. She often criticized the men who courted her, pointing out their faults. Another daily ritual for Mary Todd was reading the Illinois newspapers thoroughly so she could stay abreast of current events, especially politics. Mary Todd also called on, or visited, friends and neighbors.

The Springfield Social Scene

Mary Todd was a lively addition to the pool of eligible young ladies living in Springfield. She often visited the offices of Springfield's *Sangamon Journal*, where people met to talk politics and hear the latest news on political campaigns. She enjoyed going out, and during one particularly long stretch of heavy rain that turned the streets into mud pits and kept most ladies indoors, Mary Todd became so bored she devised a plan to make it into town. Few ladies would have attempted to negotiate the muddy, unplanked streets of Springfield in a long silk dress and slippers. But Mary Todd convinced her friend Mercy that if they threw wooden shingles in front of them as they walked, they could avoid the mud. Mary Todd and Mercy made it into town with their dresses clean, but it was impossible for them to get back the same way. Mercy stayed in town and waited for a ride in a neighbor's carriage, but Mary Todd rode home on the back of a commercial wagon. This was not appropriate behavior for a well-bred lady; in fact, it was shocking enough that one of Mary Todd's dancing partners composed a poem celebrating her adventure.

Mary Todd's energy and sense of fun made her popular, and she never lacked dancing partners. Though Mary Todd's family expected her to find a husband and eventually marry, she was in no hurry to do so. She enjoyed the unmarried world of socializing and courtship and complained that her married friends were no longer fun. "Why is it," she wrote to Mercy, "that married folks always become so serious?"[1]

Dating Abraham Lincoln

Sometime during her first year back in Springfield, Mary Todd met Abraham Lincoln, whom she had first heard of through her cousin John Todd Stuart, Lincoln's law partner. Since his arrival in 1837, Lincoln had overcome much of his shyness and had begun to participate in Springfield's social life. In 1839, he even helped organize a dance, but he was still a rough character known for wearing clothes too small for him and woodsman's boots.

The contrasts between Mary Todd and Lincoln were immediately apparent. Lincoln was as tall as

Mary Todd was short. She was as socially polished as he was awkward. He was a backwoodsman born in a Kentucky log cabin. She was brought up in one of Kentucky's most prominent families. One story handed down through the Todd family illustrates their differences. According to legend, Lincoln approached Mary Todd at a Springfield dance in 1839 and told her that he wanted to dance with her in the worst way. Mary Todd later joked that Lincoln, not exactly light on his feet, had definitely danced with her in the worst way possible.[2] Despite their differences, they were attracted to each other. They both loved to talk about politics, and they believed in the same ideals.

During the election year of 1840, Mary Todd and Abraham Lincoln grew closer. He called her by the nickname "Molly" and she called him "Mr. Lincoln." Soon they began to court. Mary Todd probably ran into Lincoln in the office of the *Sangamon Journal,* where she gathered with other political enthusiasts to hear reports on the candidates. She supported the Whig nominee William Henry Harrison; so did Lincoln. They attended the same parades and listened to the same speeches.

That year's election was one of the most exciting in recent history, featuring Whig candidate William Henry Harrison running against the Democrat Martin Van Buren. Both Mary Todd and Lincoln supported the Whig party, which campaigned for a national bank, paper currency, and humanitarian reform. In contrast, the Democrats were distrustful of reform that involved government intervention. The Democrats had also opposed the use of paper currency and the reestablishment of a national bank. In 1840, the Whig party made economic improvement a campaign issue, and with the country in a depression, the Whigs attracted voters. Voter turnout for the 1840 election was very high—80 percent of eligible voters participated—and Harrison, the Whig candidate, won.

Mary Todd's sister Elizabeth Edwards opposed Mary Todd and Abraham Lincoln's courtship. She worried that Lincoln was not the right man for Mary Todd and thought him too countrified, socially awkward, and not sufficiently educated. She considered Lincoln "the plainest looking man in Springfield" and tried to discourage Mary Todd from seeing him.[3]

But Mary Todd felt that he had great promise. Her other beaus had all been ambitious politicians, but she saw something special in Lincoln. The fact that he had no money did not stop her. In a letter to her sister, Mary Todd wrote that she would marry "a good man, with a head for position, fame and power, a man of mind with a hope and bright prospects rather than all the houses and gold in the world."[4] She was not snobbish about Lincoln's lack of money, social graces, or formal education.

Abraham Lincoln, however, was concerned about his ability to support Mary Todd as a wife. A lawyer and a member of the Illinois state legislature, Lincoln made about two thousand dollars a year, which was a good living at that time, but his income fluctuated. His earnings depended on the success of his law practice each year. He often worked with debtors and took cases on behalf of the poor. Lincoln also had no guarantee that he would be reelected to the legislature. Without wealthy parents or significant financial resources, he worried that his own earnings would not be enough to provide a comfortable lifestyle for Mary Todd.

In December 1841, Lincoln promised to escort Mary Todd to a holiday party, but he failed to arrive on time. Throughout December, Lincoln had been occupied with work and had argued nine cases before the Illinois Supreme Court that month. When he failed to arrive on time, Mary Todd grew angry and left without him. When Lincoln finally arrived at the party, he watched Mary Todd flirt with her old suitor Edwin Webb. That night, Mary Todd and Lincoln quarreled, and Mary Todd told Lincoln to leave her and not to come back. Dejected, Lincoln stopped seeing Mary Todd.

Convinced he could not be a worthy mate for her anyway, Lincoln stayed away from Mary Todd. After their breakup, he became severely depressed and missed several days of the January legislature session. His friends worried about his health. In a letter to his law partner, John Todd Stuart, Lincoln wrote:

> I am now the most miserable man living. If what I feel were equally distributed to the whole human family, there would not be one cheerful face on earth. Whether I shall be better I can not tell; I awfully forbode I shall not. To remain as I am is impossible; I must die or be better, as it appears to me.[5]

Mary Todd also suffered in Lincoln's absence. Life in Springfield became dull to her. In June 1842, she wrote to her friend Mercy, saying that the past few months "have been of *interminable* length" and that she had *"lingering regrets* over the past."[6]

In the fall of 1842, Mary Todd and Lincoln were reunited by a mutual friend, Eliza Francis, wife of the *Sangamon Journal* editor, Simeon Francis. The Francises knew both Mary Todd and Abraham Lincoln from their visits to the *Journal's* office and their mutual interest in politics. Concerned for their happiness, Mrs. Francis arranged for both Mary Todd and Lincoln to be at her house at the same time, without either of them knowing the other would be there.

Soon Mary Todd and Lincoln met again at the Francises' home. Mary Todd kept these meetings secret from her family so they could not oppose them. She and Lincoln reaffirmed their love, and politics bound them together again as they anticipated another election year in 1842, in which a new governor and legislature would be nominated and elected. In the fall of 1842, Lincoln brought Mary Todd a present—a list of election returns in the last three legislative races. Lincoln had studied these returns because he was trying to win a fourth term in the state legislature. With her own interest in politics, Mary Todd was delighted to have this present, and she saved the papers after tying them up with pink ribbon. Mary Todd grew closer to Abraham Lincoln in the election year, and their relationship grew stronger when they were attacked by one of Lincoln's political foes.

The "Rebecca" Letters

In 1841, Illinois state auditor James Shields, a Democrat, announced that Illinois would accept only gold and silver, known as specie, as payment from the people for their taxes and loans. The state would no longer accept paper currency or bank notes drawn on the Illinois state bank. Because gold and silver coins were scarce, Shields's decision would cause many people economic hardship.

Lincoln and the rest of the Whig party decided to use the controversy over specie as a vote-getting election issue. The Whigs began a series of anonymous letters to the editor of the *Sangamon Journal* that became known as the "Rebecca" letters. The letters publicized the specie issue. Abraham Lincoln authored the second "Rebecca" letter, in which he used political satire to poke fun at James Shields and the Democrats. Lincoln's satire, presented as though it were a real letter to the editor, featured a fat, old country widow named Rebecca. Rebecca complained to her neighbor Jeff that the Democrats were making it hard for poor farmers like them to pay their taxes. The satire ridiculed Shields, who insisted that his salary be paid in specie. The letter also portrayed Shields, who was known for being a lady's man, as a vain, pretentious man constantly being chased by women. "Dear girls," Lincoln had Shields say, "*it is distressing*, but I cannot marry you all. Too well I know how much you suffer; but do, *do* remember, it is not my fault that I am *so* handsome and *so* interesting."[7]

Challenged to a Duel

James Shields was very angry when the letters making fun of him appeared in print. His anger fell on Abraham Lincoln when it was discovered that Lincoln had written one of the letters. To make matters worse for Shields, one week later Mary Todd and her friend Julia Jayne collaborated to write and publish a "Rebecca" letter of their own. Their letter depicted the widow Rebecca offering herself in marriage to Shields as a means of comforting him. Mary Todd and Jayne also published a humorous wedding poem to commemorate the marriage of Rebecca and Shields.

James Shields was outraged by this public ridicule. In defense of his honor and reputation, he challenged Abraham Lincoln to a duel. At that time, dueling was considered an honorable way to settle a dispute, especially among Southerners. Lincoln agreed to the duel to protect his name and Mary Todd's. Mary Todd was familiar with dueling, because her father supported the custom. Still, she must have worried about the outcome of the Shields-Lincoln duel.

As the challenged party, Lincoln was able to choose the weapons. He selected swords because he thought they were best suited for him as a long-armed man. He practiced and was confident that he could disarm Shields without killing him. Lincoln agreed to meet Shields on Bloody Island in the middle of the Mississippi River, which was a

The Duel

Abraham Lincoln was always embarrassed by how close he came to dueling with James Shields. Mary Todd Lincoln once wrote that they had agreed never to speak of it "except," she said, "in an occasional light manner between us." Once, though, during a White House reception, a Union officer asked Lincoln if it was true that he had dueled for Mary Todd. "I do not deny it," answered the president, "but if you desire my friendship, never mention it again."[8]

traditional dueling site. Before they engaged in battle, however, Lincoln's and Shields's male friends were able to reconcile the disagreement peacefully. Afterward, Lincoln was embarrassed that the "Rebecca" letters had nearly caused a duel, and he tried never to speak of the event.

A Marriage Announcement

Shortly after the Shields affair, Mary Todd and Abraham Lincoln announced their engagement. On the rainy evening of November 4, 1842, they were married in the Edwardses' parlor by Springfield's Episcopal minister, Reverend Charles Dresser. By this time, Mary Todd's friend Mercy had married and moved away. But Mary Todd had other women to be her bridesmaids—her friend Julia Jayne, her sister Elizabeth Todd Edwards, and possibly one other female friend. Lincoln's best man was James

A Surprise Wedding

Mary Todd and Abraham Lincoln announced their wedding plans on short notice and wanted to be married immediately. Because the Todd family disapproved of her marrying Abraham Lincoln, Mary Todd was hoping that no one would have time to object. Because the wedding was organized so quickly, Mary Todd's wedding cakes were still warm at the time of the celebration.

Harvey Matheny, a good friend of his from the circuit court office. Neither the bride's nor the groom's parents attended. With her family's original disapproval of Lincoln, their breakup, and the excitement of the duel behind them, both Mary Todd and Lincoln wanted a quiet ceremony. Only a few close friends and some Todd family members attended. Lincoln gave Mary Todd a gold wedding ring he had purchased in Springfield. The words "Love Is Eternal" were engraved on it. As he gave her the ring, Lincoln did something most bridegrooms did not—he recited the law and promised to share all his worldly goods and possessions with his wife. When Lincoln finished speaking, an elderly man named Judge Brown, who was unaccustomed to such formality, spoke up. Brown reminded Lincoln that the law was implied and that he had not needed to recite it. Brown shouted loud enough for the whole wedding party to hear, "Lord Jesus Christ, God Almighty, Lincoln, the Statute fixes all that."[9]

After the wedding, Mary Todd Lincoln moved out of her sister's house into her new home, Springfield's Globe Tavern. There, she and Lincoln rented an eight- by fourteen-foot room. For four dollars a week, they were able to rent a bedroom and eat the boardinghouse meals served in the communal dining room downstairs. Moving into a boardinghouse where she did not even have her own parlor for entertaining guests was a huge change of

Abraham Lincoln posed for this photograph around the time of his marriage to Mary Todd.

lifestyle for Mary Todd Lincoln, who was used to a life of luxury.

Her circumstances had changed considerably. Without a kitchen or home to keep up, Mary Todd did not have any domestic chores to occupy her time. She was also alone for the first time in her life. Lincoln's work caused him to travel frequently, and he was away for about three months each year. Most counties in Illinois relied on itinerant, or traveling, lawyers, who went to court in each county twice a year. Mary Todd did not like it when Lincoln was gone, but working the circuit court was excellent preparation for Lincoln's political campaigns. He was able to meet many people and find out what was happening all over the state. It kept him in touch with the people of Illinois. He and the other lawyers with whom he traveled were put up overnight at different people's homes, often sleeping two to a bed.

Mary Todd Lincoln realized travel was necessary to her husband's occupation, but she always felt slighted when her husband was gone for so long and demanded a great deal of attention while he was home. The Lincolns' courtship had been stormy, and their marriage was also marked by ups and downs. Mary Todd was not afraid to speak her mind to her husband. Their Springfield neighbors recalled overhearing Mary Todd yell at her husband when she was angry. Lincoln took Mary Todd's fits of anger in stride. He tolerated her moods and often cajoled her into a sweeter temper. Mary Todd Lincoln was known in Springfield for being a lively woman with a quick and sharp tongue. While other ladies of her class considered themselves too genteel to argue for a bargain, Mary Todd Lincoln was a shrewd shopper who often haggled loudly with the grocer for better prices on fruits and vegetables.

Soon after her wedding, Mary Todd Lincoln became pregnant, and she began the long period of confinement. Pregnant women of Mary Todd Lincoln's class did not venture out in public because it was considered impolite for a lady to show her condition. As soon as a pregnancy became obvious, middle- and upper-class women began confinement, during which they would stay indoors until after the birth and up until the time their child was weaned.

Mary Todd's sisters, Elizabeth and Frances, had children of their own. They may have offered guidance and told Mary Todd what to expect during her pregnancy. Because her own mother had died in childbirth, Mary Todd Lincoln may have feared giving birth. Lincoln was with her when she delivered their first child on August 1, 1843. It was a boy, whom Mary Todd named Robert Todd Lincoln after her father. Mary Todd had no nurse or servant to help her with the baby, but one of her neighbors at the Globe Tavern did come over during the first few weeks to help her care for Robert. That fall, Lincoln moved his family into a four-room cottage on South Fourth Street in Springfield, which they were able to rent for one hundred dollars a year.

At Christmastime, Mary Todd's father came to visit the family in their new home. Robert Todd gave Mary Todd Lincoln some money and deeded her eighty acres of land in Illinois. He put Abraham Lincoln in charge of a case against some people who owed him money and told Lincoln to keep whatever money he was able to collect. This financial support made it possible for the Lincolns to buy a home by 1844. They moved into a larger cottage on one eighth of an acre at the corner of Eighth and Jackson streets in Springfield. This new home was only a few blocks from the law office where Lincoln had set up a practice with his partner, William Herndon.

Election to Congress

In 1846, Lincoln was elected to the United States Congress. As a result, he had to move to Washington, D.C., for most of the year while Congress was in session. Thrilled by her husband's election, Mary Todd decided that she and the boys, Robert and newly born Eddy Lincoln, would go with him to Washington.

Few politicians' wives at that time accompanied their husbands to Washington. Mary Todd Lincoln was an exception. Mary Todd considered herself her husband's political partner, and she planned to be

This house on Eighth and Jackson streets in Springfield, Illinois, would be the only home the Lincolns would ever own.

with him so she could offer advice and learn the ins and outs of Washington, D.C. With their Springfield house rented out, the family settled at Sprigg's Boardinghouse in the capital city. Once there, however, Mary Todd was disappointed by the bad weather and lack of friends. Unable to entertain in their boardinghouse rooms, Mary Todd met few people and spent most of her time indoors, managing the children. She was often alone, as Lincoln attended sessions during the day and Whig meetings in the evening.

In April 1848, Mary Todd returned to Lexington, Kentucky, with the children. During their separation from each other, she and Lincoln wrote frequent letters. "How much I wish instead of writing, we were together this evening," Mary Todd wrote to her husband. "I feel very sad away from you. With love I must bid you goodnight."[10] In the summer of 1848, Mary Todd and the boys met Lincoln in Washington and the family traveled back to Springfield together, going out of the way to visit Niagara Falls. When Congress reconvened, Lincoln traveled back to Washington, D.C., alone and left Mary Todd to look after Eddy, who was ill.

As the family finances improved, Mary Todd Lincoln was able to afford a servant to help her with the children, but she often went without one. Hired help was unpredictable, and the servant girls she employed did not find her an easy boss. Mary Todd was demanding and sometimes yelled when she was angry. As a result, she had a very hard time finding servants who would tolerate her temper and submit to her rules. Mary Todd especially disliked Irish girls, who represented the bulk of available hired help. One Irish girl Mary Todd hired to help with the chores went so far as to leave her window open at night to let her boyfriends climb into the Lincolns' home. This disturbed Mary Todd, especially because her husband was away so often. In a letter to her half sister, Mary Todd Lincoln wrote of her distaste for Irish servant girls, saying that Emilie

Hired Help

At her husband's request, Mary Todd Lincoln sometimes hired a woman to help out with the cooking, cleaning, and laundry. Most of these women did not last long. One was fired after she kept sneaking her boyfriend into the house at night. Others could not get along with Mary Todd Lincoln, who was known for her temper. "She always talked to us as if we had no feelings," said one of Mary Todd's hired girls, "and I was never so unhappy in my life as while living with her." But one Portuguese woman, who helped Mary Todd with the Monday washing and ironing, said Mrs. Lincoln took "no sassy talk, but if you are good to her, she is good to you and a friend to you."[11]

and her fellow Kentuckians were lucky that they did not have to "deal with the 'wild Irish,' as we housekeepers are sometimes called upon to do. . . ."[12]

In general, Mary Todd made do without domestic help, while her sisters continued to use slaves and servants. She cleaned her own house, baked her own bread, and cared for her children. She was a lenient mother, and she indulged her children with the playfulness and fun that was lacking in her own stern upbringing. Mary Todd Lincoln hosted birthday parties for her sons at a time when children's birthdays were rarely celebrated. Lincoln was also an indulgent father. "We never controlled our children much," he once said.[13] Mary Todd was adamant that their children receive good schooling. Though she missed him terribly, Robert was sent east to attend Harvard when he reached the age of sixteen.

Hosting Parties

Mary Todd Lincoln helped her husband's career by entertaining guests at their home. She gave strawberry dessert socials and dinners that featured venison, quail, wild turkey, and other fresh game. Sometimes she invited fellow Presbyterian Church members over for tea. She also helped "Mr. Lincoln," as she always called him, by teaching him the finer points of social etiquette, such as how to converse properly at a dinner party and how to use the correct utensils for each course. By the 1850s, Lincoln's successful law practice allowed the couple

Mary Todd Lincoln served as a gracious hostess, doing her part to help advance her husband's political career.

to entertain more lavishly, and his political aspirations made it necessary for them to entertain frequently. Fortunately, Mary Todd Lincoln excelled as a hostess. She loved to entertain, and on more formal occasions she even greeted her guests in French, which lent an air of high culture to her parties. Mary Todd also loved to dress up, and she carefully chose the fabrics and decorations for her more formal dresses.

Mary Todd was a good hostess, and her friends found her charming, but she had a hard time being polite to anyone she did not like. One such person was her husband's law partner, William Herndon, toward whom Mary Todd felt a lifelong dislike. He would one day become one of her biggest enemies. Mary Todd had never cared for Herndon, but her argument with him began when, in her eyes, he insulted her on the dance floor by saying that her waltzing was like the "gliding of a snake."[14] Mary Todd had such a fiery temper that she was never able to forgive an insult, and she never again danced with Herndon at any function. In fact, she banned him from any party in her house, even though he was her husband's law partner. Given Mary Todd's frequent entertaining, Herndon's absence at the Lincoln parties was conspicuous. He most likely felt slighted by Mary Todd Lincoln for this treatment and never said a kind word about her. In later life, he did all he could to disparage her.

Despite the hostility between Mary Todd Lincoln and William Herndon, the Lincolns' position required them to entertain often. To make the Lincoln home larger and better suited for company, Mary Todd eventually supervised the building of an addition onto the house at Eighth and Jackson. She financed the addition by selling the eighty acres her father had given her after her marriage. The Lincoln home was now much grander, with four bedrooms upstairs and a large parlor downstairs. As a hostess and as a political strategist, Mary Todd Lincoln intended to do all that was in her power to help her husband rise politically.

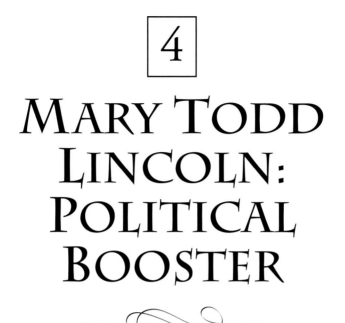

4

MARY TODD LINCOLN: POLITICAL BOOSTER

Whenever political prospects seemed to dampen for Abraham Lincoln, Mary Todd did all she could to improve her husband's career. In 1846, Lincoln had opposed going to war with Mexico. He could not justify a war to expand United States territory in the Southwest, particularly because any new territory might become a slave state, and he opposed the expansion of slavery. Lincoln's opposition to the war made him unpopular, even among other Whigs. The United States won its war against Mexico, gaining the territory of California, New Mexico, present-day Nevada, Utah, and Arizona. The addition of the new territories was politically popular and hurt Lincoln's position.

Determined to help her husband's prospects, Mary Todd advised Lincoln, wrote letters to key individuals on Lincoln's behalf, and recommended him for certain positions. Mary Todd Lincoln wrote to Whig President Zachary Taylor to recommend Lincoln for the vacant position of commissioner of the Land Office. She also wrote to prominent Whigs in the Midwest, asking them to support Lincoln for the office. She even signed her letters "A. Lincoln."

Despite these efforts, Lincoln did not get the position. President Taylor offered him the position of governor of the Oregon Territory instead. Lincoln might have accepted this offer if Mary Todd had not been against it. She felt his political chances as a Whig in Oregon—a Democratic territory—were poor and that he would do better to remain in Illinois. In addition, the trip to the Oregon Territory was a difficult one, and Eddy Lincoln was sick. Mary Todd also did not relish the idea of living in the wilderness. So the Lincolns remained in Springfield.

Little Eddy Lincoln, born in 1846, had been sick for most of the first years of his life. In 1850, he died of tuberculosis, an infectious disease of the lungs, which was the most common cause of death in America at the time. He was only three and a half years old. Both Mary Todd and her husband grieved for a long time. According to one friend of the family, it was Lincoln who finally encouraged Mary Todd to move past her grief, reminding her, "Eat, Mary, for we must live."[1] Soon after Eddy's death in 1850, Mary Todd Lincoln gave birth to another son, named William, or "Willie." Three years later, Thomas "Tad" Lincoln was born, which completed the Lincoln family.

Conflict Over Slavery

While Abraham and Mary Todd Lincoln tried to chart his political future, the issues of territorial expansion and slavery completely changed the American political landscape. The settlement of new western territories had raised the question of whether slavery would be allowed there. Supporters of slavery wanted to promote its expansion into the territories. Opponents of slavery wanted to stop its spread. Attempting to please both proslavery and antislavery factions, Senator Henry Clay, a friend of Mary Todd Lincoln's from Kentucky, and Illinois Senator Stephen Douglas, Mary Todd's former beau, created the Compromise of 1850. This compromise admitted California to the Union as a free state but left the New Mexico and Utah territories open to "popular sovereignty." In other words, settlers in those territories would get to decide whether or not slavery would be allowed. The compromise also included a strong fugitive slave law to assist in returning escaped slaves to their owners.

The Compromise of 1850 did not resolve the issue of slavery's expansion. Senator Stephen

Douglas went on to propose the Kansas-Nebraska bill, which allowed popular sovereignty in the Kansas and Nebraska territories. Despite great opposition, the bill became law in 1854. By allowing popular sovereignty in the Kansas and Nebraska territories, the bill violated the Missouri Compromise of 1820, which had outlawed slavery in all of the Louisiana Purchase north of the 36th parallel. The passage of the Kansas-Nebraska Act opened lands that had previously been closed to slavery. It caused an outrage among those who opposed slavery's expansion. One of the chief opponents of the Kansas-Nebraska Act was Abraham Lincoln, who believed the Founding Fathers had intended to curb the spread of slavery so that it would eventually end.

The debate over slavery caused the old two-party political system to fall apart as both Whigs and Democrats switched parties to align themselves either for or against slavery's expansion. Politics began to express sectional interests: Many Southerners joined the Democrats and were proslavery, whereas many Northerners, who opposed the expansion of slavery into the territories, formed the new Republican party in 1854. The Whig party disintegrated as proslavery Whigs joined the Democrats and antislavery Whigs, along with abolitionists and Free-Soilers, joined the Republicans. (Free-Soilers were people who did not necessarily consider slavery wrong, but wanted to prevent it from spreading.)

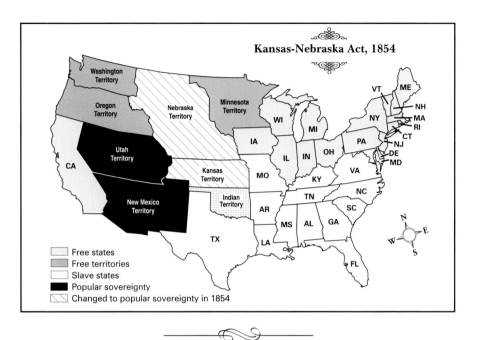

Kansas-Nebraska Act, 1854

Free states
Free territories
Slave states
Popular sovereignty
Changed to popular sovereignty in 1854

The Kansas-Nebraska Act of 1854 heightened national tensions over slavery. It also led to the formation of the new Republican party, of which Abraham Lincoln would become the leader.

Their motto became "Free Soil, Free Labor, Free Men." Both sides looked to politics to further their cause.

The Kansas-Nebraska Act, however, had more than political effects. It also caused an all-out mad dash by both antislavery and proslavery groups to settle the new territories with their supporters. Each side wanted to gain ground in the battle over the expansion of slavery. The opposing interests often clashed violently in the territories. The violence even spilled over to the floor of the United States Senate. Massachusetts Senator Charles

Sumner blamed the violence in Kansas on proslavery forces, including South Carolina Senator Andrew Butler. Butler's nephew, Congressman Preston Brooks, attacked Sumner on the floor of the Senate, clubbing him over the head with a cane until he collapsed.

The Lincolns knew firsthand about the violence the debate over slavery could cause. Mary Todd's childhood friend Cassius Clay, who ran an abolitionist newspaper, had been attacked by a violent proslavery mob who destroyed his printing press in Lexington, Kentucky. When Clay spoke in Springfield in 1854, he denounced the spread of slavery through territorial expansion. Mary Todd and Abraham Lincoln attended his speech, which was considered so radical it was not allowed to take place in the state house. Clay, Lincoln, and their fellow Republicans believed themselves to be progressive, freedom-loving, and industrious people compared with what they considered the backward, feudal South. Abraham Lincoln seemed to be the ideal hardworking man who could seize opportunity and become successful, despite humble log-cabin origins. As a result, he would soon become a symbol for the Republican party.

Lincoln's politics often put Mary Todd in the position of having to explain herself to her Kentucky family. Some of her relatives, including Mary Todd's own half sister Emilie Todd Helm, who had married into a proslavery Kentucky family, openly questioned

Lincoln's politics. Though Mary Todd supported her husband's politics, she tried to justify Lincoln's anti-slavery views to her family. In an 1856 letter to Emilie Todd Helm, Mary Todd insisted that her husband did not oppose slavery where it existed, but that he did oppose slavery's expansion into the West. Mary Todd Lincoln's own views on slavery were similar; she was not opposed to the institution of slavery, but she did not want to see it spread to new territory.

Lincoln Seeks a Seat in the Senate

In a now-famous speech given in 1858, Abraham Lincoln expressed his beliefs on the fate of the Union and the issue of slavery:

> I do not expect the union to be dissolved—I do not expect the House to fall—but I do expect it to cease to be divided. It will become all one thing or all the other. Either the opponents of slavery will arrest the further spread of it, and place it where the public mind shall rest in the belief that it is in the course of ultimate extinction; or its advocates will push it forward, till it shall become alike lawful in all the States, old as well as new, North as well as South.[2]

In 1855, Lincoln lost the Republican nomination for Senate to his ally Lyman Trumball, the husband of Mary Todd Lincoln's long-time friend Julia Jayne. Although Lincoln had received forty-five votes and Trumball only five, Lincoln conceded his votes and passed his support to Trumball to show party unity. Mary Todd was horrified. She felt Trumball should have given his five votes to Lincoln, not the other way around. She made the political defeat a personal one and resented Julia Jayne for not convincing Trumball to throw his support to Lincoln. Mary Todd assumed that other women had as much influence over their husbands' political lives as she did. This was not often the case. Mary Todd felt betrayed by Julia Jayne, and she broke off their friendship. Mary Todd Lincoln's dispute with Julia Jayne set a lifelong precedent for losing friends over politics. Unlike her husband, Mary Todd always took defeat personally, and she was not a good loser.

In 1858, however, Lincoln finally won the Republican nomination for the United States Senate. He and his rival for the Senate slot, Democrat Stephen Douglas, began a series of debates over the issue of slavery in the territories. The now-famous Lincoln-Douglas debates took place at various spots in Illinois. For the most part, Mary Todd Lincoln stayed home, while Lincoln traveled the state, repeating his theme: "A house divided against itself cannot stand. I believe this government cannot endure permanently half-slave and half-free."[3] In opposition, Douglas campaigned for popular sovereignty and accused Lincoln of wanting to extend freedom to slaves. Despite his eloquent speeches, Lincoln lost the Senate seat to Douglas in 1858. Because he had put his law practice on hold to pursue the Senate seat, he faced a severe lack of money.

However, the Senate race had gained him a national reputation. By 1860, Lincoln was being considered for the Republican nomination for president.

A Nomination for the Presidency

Mary Todd Lincoln had always predicted that her husband would be president someday, and she certainly encouraged him in this endeavor. By 1860, it seemed likely that he would be a candidate. In February 1860, he delivered a speech at the Cooper Union in New York, which made him known to eastern Republicans. Lincoln's prospects were further boosted when the Republican convention was held in Chicago, and he won his party's nomination. As soon as Lincoln heard the news, he hurried home to inform his wife. Mary Todd Lincoln, who had always craved attention, was now, at age forty-two, going to get more attention than any other woman in the country.

Overnight, Mary Todd Lincoln became public property. After her husband's nomination for president, Mary Todd was surrounded

Abraham Lincoln was nominated as the Republican candidate for president in the 1860 election.

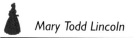

by the press and people of all kinds who wanted to know more about Abraham Lincoln's wife and family. Unlike the wives of most other politicians, Mary Todd Lincoln was outgoing and opinionated. She did not shy away from discussing politics. In fact, Mary Todd took an active role in helping her husband get elected. She embarked on more letter-writing campaigns, worked to correct misunderstandings about his political views and his record, and discussed possible patronage positions for those who helped Lincoln's campaign.

Lincoln ran on a Republican platform that did not oppose slavery where it already existed, but did oppose the expansion of slavery into the territories. The Democratic party split in the election. The Northern Democrats nominated Stephen Douglas, Mary's former beau; the Southern Democrats nominated John C. Breckinridge of Kentucky; and a pro-Union group calling itself the Constitutional Union party nominated a candidate from Tennessee named John Bell. On November 6, 1860, fifty-one-year-old Abraham Lincoln was elected president of the United States. He first heard the news in Springfield's telegraph office and ran home to announce, "Mary, Mary, we are elected!"[4]

5

FIRST LADY

Mary Todd Lincoln's life changed forever after her husband's election. As soon as Lincoln won the presidential election in November 1860, he began to receive death threats. Drawings of Lincoln's body hanging from a noose arrived with the family's mail. Letters with skulls and crossbones drawn on them arrived, addressed to Mary Todd Lincoln. They warned her that her husband could be killed if he took office. These messages came from Southerners who were angry that an antislavery Republican had become president. A Virginia newspaper echoed the sentiments of other Southern papers and called Lincoln's election "the greatest evil that has ever befallen this country."[1] For the first time, the members of the Lincoln family had to be concerned for their safety.

In December 1860, more than two months before Lincoln was due to take office, South Carolina, the fiercest proslavery state, seceded from, or left, the Union. Upset over the election of Lincoln, who refused to allow the expansion of slavery into the territories, South Carolina declared itself independent from the federal government. Withdrawing from the Union, South Carolina formed its own government. To defend Southern rights and the Southern way of life, which revolved around slavery, ten more Southern states followed South Carolina in seceding from the Union, and together they formed the Confederate States of America.

The rest of the nation looked to Lincoln to find a way of preserving the Union and to bring reconciliation between the states of the Union and the departed Southern states. Despite the mounting pressure on her husband and the barrage of death threats, Mary Todd Lincoln was not discouraged. In January 1861, one month before Lincoln's inauguration, Mary Todd decided that she could not go to Washington without new clothes. There were jokes circulating in the east that she and her husband were backwoods pioneers, and she intended to show the world that the Lincolns were not hicks. To find clothes appropriate for the wife of a president, Mary

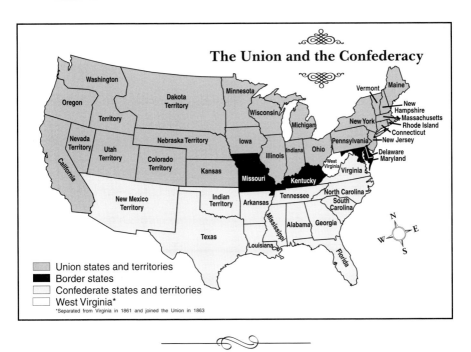

The Union and the Confederacy

Union states and territories
Border states
Confederate states and territories
West Virginia*
*Separated from Virginia in 1861 and joined the Union in 1863

Shortly after Abraham Lincoln's election, Southern states seceded from the Union to form their own nation, the Confederate States of America. This map shows how the states were divided.

Todd Lincoln traveled by train to New York, where she shopped for dress material and was fitted for a new wardrobe. Enjoying her prominence, Mary Todd even held a ladies' tea at the Astor Hotel. Some people, however, including her friend Mercy, felt that Mary Todd's carefree behavior was unbecoming at a time when the country was going through a crisis.

The Lincolns Move to Washington, D.C.

When Mary Todd returned to Springfield, the Lincolns sold most of their household possessions and packed their trunks for their move to Washington. In February 1861, Abraham Lincoln and his oldest son, Robert, were given a send-off by the town of Springfield. They began their journey to Washington in a special four-car train decorated with red, white, and blue swags. At first, security concerns prevented Mary Todd Lincoln and the two younger boys from traveling with Lincoln. But in the end it was decided that their presence might help deter an assassin, so Mary Todd, Willie, and Tad boarded the presidential train the next day. As the train made its way east, citizens lined up along the railroad tracks to see the new president and his family. In larger towns, the train stopped and Lincoln gave speeches. People cheered and asked to see the Lincolns' children. With news that there might be trouble in Baltimore, Lincoln's advisors encouraged him to change his itinerary and travel alone on a night train from Pennsylvania to the capital instead. Mary Todd and the boys rode the other, decoy, train, on which Lincoln was believed to be traveling. When they reached Baltimore, the crowd was indeed hostile and jeering. People yelled at Mary Todd Lincoln, demanding to see her husband, whom they called the "Black Ape" and that "bloody Republican."[2]

Reunited in Washington, the Lincolns stayed in a hotel until the inauguration, which was scheduled for March 4, 1861. The inauguration took place as

Abraham Lincoln delivered his inaugural address beneath the edifice of the Capitol, still under construction.

planned, along with the traditional ball, at which Mary Todd Lincoln starred. The newspapers, noting her hospitality and liveliness, called her gracious and charming. Mary Todd Lincoln was unlike any other First Lady the nation had seen. Whereas many First Ladies had hated the public life that came with the job, Mary Todd enjoyed the attention she received and the role she could play. Yet Mary Todd Lincoln did not like to be called an ambitious woman. Though she was very ambitious, she was also aware that it was considered unladylike to be that way. Thus Mary Todd was annoyed when *The New York Times* quite accurately reported, "Mrs. Lincoln is making and unmaking the political fortunes of men and is similar to Queen Elizabeth in her statesman-like tastes."[3]

Renovating the White House

From the start, Mary Todd Lincoln was determined that the White House, which she found shockingly decrepit, would become a place of great beauty. She set out to replace its broken furniture, torn curtains, mismatched china, and worn rugs with new items that were in keeping with the dignity of the office of the president. Because the White House was considered American public property, anyone could wander into its downstairs rooms. Visitors sometimes stole things or cut off pieces of the curtains as souvenirs. A French prince who visited the Lincolns remarked that people went right into the White

House "as if entering a café."[4] As a result, the White House resembled an ugly old hotel more than an executive mansion. Since each president was allowed twenty thousand dollars for improvements to the White House, Mary Todd Lincoln immediately took charge of this money. With the commissioner of public buildings, William Wood, along to approve her purchases, Mary Todd Lincoln and her cousin Elizabeth Todd Grimsley shopped for the White House at stores in New York and Philadelphia.

Perhaps Mary Todd compensated for years of her necessary penny-pinching in Springfield and shopped too much, overspending her allowance. Her expensive shopping excursions became a subject for gossip. Though Commissioner Wood had allowed her to overspend, Mary Todd received all the blame. Many people felt that the money being spent to improve the White House would be better off going toward paying for the Civil War, which had begun just one month into Lincoln's presidency.

The War Between the States

On April 12, 1861, Confederate soldiers from the seceded states fired on Fort Sumter, a garrison for federal troops located in South Carolina's Charleston Harbor. The bombardment of the fort marked the beginning of the Civil War. Lincoln called on federal, or Union, soldiers to put down the Southern uprising. This, however, only encouraged the South

The Civil War began when the Confederates fired on Fort Sumter in Charleston Harbor, South Carolina.

to rebel. Determined to defend their territory against what they considered Northern aggression, Southern men joined the Confederate Army by the thousands. Soon the Union and Confederate armies were clashing on the battlefield. Men began to die; families were turned against each other, some fighting for the North, others for the South. Some of Mary Todd Lincoln's own family joined the Confederate Army to fight the government led by her husband.

As the broken nation reacted to the crisis, Lincoln worked long hours in the White House. He met with advisors and listened to soldiers' stories of what was happening on the battlefront. The city of

Washington became a military encampment. Though Union soldiers camped on the nearby Potomac River to protect the capital, Confederate flags flew within eyesight of the White House. Southerners in Washington society broke off relations with the Lincolns. The city was polarized. Tensions ran high. Then rumors came that the Confederate Army was going to invade Washington, D.C. Residents poured out of the city, leaving it almost deserted. Hearing reports that at least one

At the start of the Civil War, many people feared for the safety of the nation's capital city. Here, soldiers are seen protecting the White House from a possible Confederate attack.

Confederate regiment planned to occupy the White House and kidnap the president's family, General Winfield Scott and other officials begged Mary Todd Lincoln to take her children and leave for a safer place. But Mary Todd steadfastly refused to abandon the capital. As long as her husband stayed, she planned to stay. By carrying on as usual in Washington, D.C., Mary Todd Lincoln demonstrated her unwillingness to submit to Confederate threats. So Mary Todd adjusted to living with Union troops camped out in her home, and she adapted herself to a wartime role. Sometimes with her

First Lady Fashions

Mary Todd Lincoln believed the First Lady should dress elaborately, and she chose white or brightly colored gowns with plunging necklines and giant hoopskirts. One of her dresses required twenty-five yards of material. Mary Todd Lincoln usually wore fresh flowers in her hair to complete her look. But not every guest of the White House appreciated her stately appearance. Some felt that at age forty-three, Mary Todd Lincoln dressed too youthfully. Oregon Senator James Nesmith, accustomed to more simple country dressing, complained to his wife about "Mrs. Lincoln and her sorry show of skin and bones. She had her bosom on exhibition, a flower pot on her head—There was a train of silk dragging on the floor behind her of several yards in length."[5]

husband and sometimes on her own, Mary Todd Lincoln reviewed troops, and later, she comforted wounded soldiers in army hospitals.

Yet, in the midst of war, Mary Todd continued to shop for the White House. Her lavish wartime purchases became the subject of slanderous talk, and all of Washington whispered about her fancy dresses. In less than a year, Mary Todd had overspent the twenty thousand dollars that was meant to last the four years of the president's term. President Lincoln was angry with Mary Todd for creating such a scene. He told her that her expensive shopping trips would "stink" in the land, and he fired Commissioner Wood for failing to perform his duty.[6] To make amends with her husband, Mary Todd looked for ways to scrape expenses off the White House budget. She economized by downsizing the staff and selling the old furniture. Mary Todd did not want to pay the debts with her husband's salary, because she was trying to save as much as possible.

White House Hostess

One of the president's major expenses, paid out of his own pocket, was the cost of entertaining. The Lincolns had to pay for the catering at all White House events. Traditionally, the White House held receptions twice a week in the winter and spring so visitors could interact with the president. As many as four thousand people came to these affairs, and they expected to be fed. It was at these receptions

Charming Her Visitors

Massachusetts historian George Bancroft found Mary Todd Lincoln charming when he met her at a White House reception:

> *She tells me she is a conservative, repudiates the idea that her secessionist brothers can have any influence on her, spoke of the Herald as a paper friendly to Mr. Lincoln, . . . discussed eloquently the review the other day. . . . She told what orders she had given for renewing the White House and her elegant fitting up of Mr. Lincoln's room—, her love of flowers . . . and ended with giving me a gracious invitation to repeat my visit and saying that she would send me a bouquet. I came home entranced.*[7]

that Mary Todd Lincoln shined. While many in the president's Cabinet made excuses to avoid receptions, with their long receiving lines and thousands of handshakes, Mary Todd Lincoln was a tireless hostess. She would stay up all night with guests and then soak her husband's hand when the party was over because he was blistered from shaking so many hands. Most visitors found her charming. Those who sought favors from the president often tried to enlist her in their behalf. Trying to win her influence, they sometimes gave her gifts of jewels, clothing, and even a carriage and horses. However, if they did not get what they wanted from her husband, they might later submit a bill for these "gifts." Never sure whether something was a gift or not, Mary Todd sometimes accrued debts on items that were supposedly "given" to her.

The president of the United States is able to appoint a number of people to Cabinet posts and other positions in his administration. Often, the president chooses supporters who have helped his campaign for these appointments, which are called patronage positions. After his election, Lincoln was bombarded with requests from his supporters for patronage positions. In particular, many of Mary Todd Lincoln's relatives clamored for appointments. At Mary Todd's request, Lincoln gave positions to some of her Todd relatives, including two of her brothers-in-law.

For the most part, however, Mary Todd's role as Lincoln's political advisor had ended. Unlike their Springfield years, Lincoln was now surrounded by official advisors and secretaries who helped him devise policy. Mary Todd had a new role of her own to play as the nation's First Lady, but she had lost much of her power to affect her husband's decision making. Mary Todd remained politically interested but was no longer able to participate as freely in her husband's politics. Nevertheless, she continued to encourage her husband to appoint those whom she favored and pass over those whom she did not. Mary

Todd's influence caused Lincoln's advisors to secretly refer to her as "Mrs. President," and the *New York World* dubbed her the "Presidentess."[8]

Traveling to the Front Lines

As First Lady, Mary Todd Lincoln's job and public appearances were not limited to the White House. She frequently traveled to perform wartime duties. Throughout the war, Mary Todd traveled with Lincoln to Union Army campsites on the front lines, where they would review the troops and try to raise morale. A proud woman, Mary Todd enjoyed her public appearances, and she did not like to be upstaged by other women while conducting official business.

Mary Todd Lincoln was an active, highly visible First Lady. She constantly made public appearances and often visited Union soldiers in hospitals, where she wrote letters for the wounded men. Mary Todd Lincoln also took up the cause of the thousands of freed and escaped Virginia slaves, known as contrabands of war, who had come north and were now living in shantytowns in the nation's capital. Her friend and seamstress Elizabeth Keckley, a freed black woman, encouraged Mary Todd Lincoln to do something for these people, who lacked jobs and money. Many of them did not even have basic necessities. As Mary Todd wrote in 1862, "These immense number of Contrabands are suffering intensely, many without bed covering and having to use any bits of carpeting to cover themselves—many

A Short Temper
In March 1865, Mary Todd Lincoln went with her husband to help review the Union troops and raise morale. Mary Todd discovered that the wives of two officers had ridden beside her husband on horseback while she rode far behind them in a carriage. She grew enraged that she had been upstaged by other women. According to one officer who was present,

> Mrs. Lincoln repeatedly attacked her husband in the presence of officers because of Mrs. Griffin and Mrs. Ord [the women who had ridden with her husband]. He bore it as Christ might have done with an expression of pain and sadness that cut one to the heart, but with supreme calmness and dignity. He pleaded with eyes and tones, till she turned on him like a tigress and then he walked away hiding that noble ugly face so that we might not catch the full expression of its misery.[9]

Afterward, Mary Todd was very embarrassed by her outburst and apologized to her husband for her behavior.

dying of want."[10] Mary Todd Lincoln and Elizabeth Keckley worked together to raise money for the Contraband Relief Society, which provided food, blankets, and other items for those in need.

In addition to renovating the White House, hosting receptions, securing patronage positions, making public appearances, and raising funds, Mary Todd

The Armory Square Hospital in Washington, D.C. Mary Todd Lincoln visited Washington hospitals like this one, bringing food and cheer to the wounded.

Visiting the Wounded

Two or three times a week, Mary Todd Lincoln visited the foul-smelling soldiers' hospital in Washington, D.C., where wounded Union soldiers lay, either dying or recovering. Despite the risk of infection, Mary Todd Lincoln came to visit the sick men, often bringing fresh flowers and baskets of fruit from the White House, as well as little presents. Sometimes she would bring food specially prepared in the White House kitchen. Mary Todd Lincoln chatted with the soldiers and cheered them up. She also wrote to the mothers of soldiers who were too sick to write. Many of the soldiers did not even know who she was, because she came alone and without fanfare. One recovering soldier for whom she had written a letter did not realize he had been talking with the First Lady until he returned home and his mother showed him the letter she had received, which was signed "Mrs. Abraham Lincoln."

Lincoln was a wife and mother. She was Lincoln's helpmate through all the Union defeats and losses that accompanied the Civil War. At the end of a long day, the two would often meet to spend some quiet time together and to discuss the day's events. Mary Todd and her husband also devoted a great deal of

time to their children, who were the sensations of the White House.

A Family in the White House

Americans had never seen children like Tad and Willie Lincoln in the White House. While their older brother, Robert, was studying at Harvard, Tad and Willie, ages eight and ten, terrorized the White House staff. Together with Bud and Holly Taft, sons of the Lincolns' Washington friends, the boys formed a pack that roamed the executive mansion freely and frequently created disturbances. They brought their pet goats into the White House, interrupted Cabinet meetings, and sold candy to White House visitors.

Mary Todd and Abraham Lincoln believed in letting their boys have fun, though the White House staff may have disagreed with their permissive approach to parenting. Sometimes President Lincoln wrestled with his sons and their friends, and the young boys delighted in pinning the president's arms and legs to the floor. Mary Todd Lincoln occasionally allowed the boys to attend state dinners. Willie and Tad once starred in their own White House circus, charging five cents' admission to any members of the public who wanted to attend. Another time, they tried to fire a cannon from the roof of the White House.

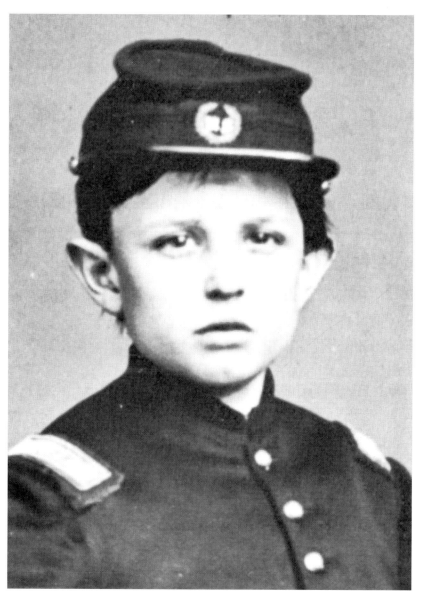

Tad Lincoln caused a lot of commotion in the White House. He is seen here in his Union officer's uniform, specially commissioned for him around 1864.

Pardoning the Presidential Turkey

A friend of the Lincolns' sent a live turkey to the White House for the family's Christmas dinner in 1863. Because the turkey arrived several weeks in advance of the holiday, little Tad Lincoln had a chance to become friendly with the bird, whom he named Jack. Tad took excellent care of Jack, who began to follow him around the White House. The day before Christmas, Tad, in tears, burst into the president's office, interrupting a Cabinet meeting. He sobbed that the White House cook was about to kill Jack, and he begged his father to save the turkey's life. Lincoln reminded Tad that Jack had been given to them to eat on Christmas Day. Tad continued to sob. "I can't help it," he said. "He's a good turkey and I don't want him killed."[11] So President Lincoln wrote a pardon for Jack on one of his cards and gave it to Tad to show the cook. Jack's life was spared, and today the White House continues to provide pardons for the annual presidential turkey.

In 1862, the White House grew quiet when both Willie and Tad became sick with typhoid fever. They contracted the disease from the White House drinking water, which was drawn from the Potomac River. The Potomac had been contaminated by the sewage of the Union Army camped beside it. Tad survived, but Willie died from the illness.

Unable to overcome her grief, Mary Todd Lincoln stayed in bed for months after Willie's death. She wore black mourning clothes for over a year and could not bear to enter either the room where Willie had died or the room where his body had been embalmed. Abraham Lincoln, himself distraught, encouraged her to recover so that they could go on with their lives.

With the help of her close friend Elizabeth Keckley, Mary Todd recovered somewhat. To deal with Willie's death, she began to experiment with spiritualism, the belief that the dead could be contacted by the living. Elizabeth Keckley practiced spiritualism as a means of contacting her son, who had died in the Civil War, and she encouraged Mary Todd in her efforts.

Spiritualism and Premonitions

Spiritualists believe that the spirits of the dead can contact the living with the help of a medium, who acts as an interpreter between the spirit and physical worlds. Spiritualism had been popular in the United States since the 1840s, and by the 1860s, millions of Americans believed in it. With the help of spiritualist friends, many of whom were socially prominent in Washington, Mary Todd Lincoln held seances to try to contact Willie and Eddy Lincoln. She believed that they could hear her and that they appeared to her at night. These beliefs gave Mary Todd great comfort.

Despite its popularity, spiritualism was not considered a respectable practice by many people, and churches opposed it. By participating in spiritualist activities, Mary Todd invited criticism. In addition to practicing spiritualism, she may also have tried to interpret her dreams. Mary Todd sometimes had premonitions, or dreams that later came true. She had a premonition that Abraham Lincoln would become president, and he did. But she also had a premonition that he would be killed. Understandably, Mary Todd would have wanted to learn more about this dream of hers.

Lincoln himself often had nightmares and disturbing premonitions, which he shared with his wife. During his re-election campaign in 1864, he had a dream that on election day in 1860 he was sitting in his Springfield bedroom. There, he saw not one, but two reflections of his face in the bedroom mirror, with one reflection much paler than the other. Mary Todd believed this meant that he would be elected twice, but that he would not live to finish the second term. When Lincoln was elected to a second term in 1864, Mary Todd was afraid there would be an assassination attempt. In the summer of 1864, while Lincoln was riding his horse alone at night in Washington, a bullet was fired at him. It went through the top of his tall stovepipe hat and he was unharmed. After that, his security guards warned him not to go out alone. Lincoln was aware

Like his wife, Abraham Lincoln had strange dreams and premonitions. Among them was a dream that he might not live to complete his second term.

of the danger he faced but believed "I shall live til my work is done and no earthly power can prevent it. And then, it doesn't matter, so that I am ready, and that I ever mean to be."[12]

In the spring of 1865, Lincoln described another one of his dreams to Mary Todd. In the dream, he heard people crying in the White House, and in the East Room he saw a coffin. When he asked a soldier standing by whose body it was, the soldier replied that it was the president, who had been killed by an assassin.

The Assassination of President Lincoln

On April 9, 1865, General Robert E. Lee surrendered his Confederate Army, marking the approaching end of the Civil War. With the immense relief that came as peace approached, Lincoln told Mary Todd that he was happier than he had ever been.[13] But just as the president was making plans to aid the war-torn South, the Lincolns' worst premonitions came true.

On their way to the theater on the evening of April 14, 1865, Mary Todd and Abraham Lincoln rode alone in their carriage, making plans for the future. At Ford's Theatre in Washington, D.C., they sat in a special box seat decorated with red, white, and blue swags while they watched a comedy called *Our American Cousin.* An hour and a half into the play, as the Lincolns held hands, a man named John

On April 14, 1865, John Wilkes Booth shot Abraham Lincoln in the head while the president and First Lady watched a play. The assassin then ran across the stage of Ford's Theatre as he made his escape.

Wilkes Booth crept into the theater box and shot President Lincoln in the back of the head.

Mary Todd followed the men who carried her unconscious husband out of Ford's Theatre to a room at a nearby boardinghouse. Unconscious, the president lay on a bed too short for his six-foot four-inch frame while doctors, government officials, and friends crowded next to him. Robert Lincoln was also present. Mary Todd Lincoln kissed her husband, who never woke up again. Early the next morning, after an all-night vigil around his bed, Abraham Lincoln died. He was the first United States president to die at the hand of an assassin. Some believed that Mary Todd Lincoln, who would never stop grieving her husband's death, died that day, too.

6

WIDOWHOOD

The impact of Abraham Lincoln's assassination on Mary Todd Lincoln's life was enormous. Overnight, her life changed forever. She was no longer the country's First Lady. Though she had the sympathy of the entire nation, it was little consolation for the loss of her husband. Until her death, she dressed in full mourning costume—heavy black crepe dresses and a black bonnet with a black veil. She only wrote letters on stationery with a black edge.[1] Mourning usually lasted only a year, but Mary Todd Lincoln never stopped letting the world know that she was Abraham Lincoln's widow. She never went to the theater again.

After her husband's death, Mary Todd Lincoln spent the rest of her life wearing mourning clothes like these.

Shortly after Lincoln's death, the conspirators who had plotted to kill the president were tried and hanged.

In the week following Lincoln's death, the whole nation mourned. Letters of condolence from around the world arrived at the White House. The New York Stock Exchange closed down out of respect for the president. Mary Todd Lincoln had to endure the laying out of Lincoln's body in the East Room of the White House, where the public could see their president one last time. Long lines of people formed to pay their last respects and peer into the open coffin where the president's body lay. Overcome with grief, Mary Todd was unable to attend the funeral,

and she stayed upstairs in bed while it took place. After an elaborate state funeral, Lincoln's body was placed on a funeral train draped in black and bound for Springfield, Illinois. The train traveled through cities, including Baltimore, Harrisburg, Philadelphia, New York, Albany, Buffalo, Cleveland, Columbus, Indianapolis, and Chicago, as it worked its way back to Springfield, Illinois. At every town in between, people lined the tracks to catch a glimpse of the funeral train and to bid a final farewell to their fallen leader.

Mary Todd wanted to keep the family's graves together. She had their son Willie's remains exhumed from the Georgetown cemetery and placed on the train with his father's. She wanted Lincoln and Willie to join Eddy Lincoln's body in the Springfield family plot. But the citizens of Springfield had their own burial plans for Lincoln. They wanted to bury him in a public monument in the middle of town. Mary Todd had to fight her old neighbors for the right to bury her husband in a private family plot at Oak Ridge Cemetery. The fact that she had to argue for the right to her husband's body reflected her new position.

Overnight, Mary Todd Lincoln's status had plummeted. Gone were her privileges as First Lady. The whole nation was mourning the loss of its president, but in the meantime, Mary Todd was expected to pack her things and move out of the

White House to make way for the new president. Prostrate with grief, Mary Todd was unable or unwilling to do this. She lay in bed in the White House for over a month, refusing most company. She became ill. Newly sworn-in President Andrew Johnson waited for Mary Todd Lincoln and her children to leave. In the meantime, he worked out of a room in the Treasury Department. Mary Todd resented Johnson and even harbored suspicions that he was involved in the assassination plot. She replayed the details of the shooting over and over again in her head, and every loud sound reminded her of the gunshot.[2]

Robert and Tad tried to comfort their mother. Mary Todd eventually managed to prepare for their departure, packing all of the family's belongings into trunks with the help of Elizabeth Keckley. Judge David Davis, whom Robert Lincoln had appointed to handle Abraham Lincoln's estate, encouraged Mary Todd to return to the family house in Springfield. But Mary Todd felt Springfield held too many memories and that it would be too painful to return there.

Mary Todd Lincoln decided to move with the boys and Elizabeth Keckley to a Chicago hotel. Though many called on her there, she chose to see only a few individuals. Those who saw her reported that she was obsessed with the details of Lincoln's assassination. Mary Todd blamed herself for her

Andrew Johnson became president after Abraham Lincoln's death. Mary Todd Lincoln disliked the new president and even thought he might have been involved in the plot to kill her husband.

husband's death because she had encouraged his political aspirations. As she had exclaimed after the shooting, "Oh, My God, and have I given my husband to die."[3]

A Loss of Prestige

The trappings of the presidency gave way to a more realistic life. No longer able to make grand purchases with the help of obliging merchants, unlimited credit, and a White House expense account, Mary Todd Lincoln had to reduce her expenses and live on a modest income. She enrolled Tad in school. Now a grown man, Robert found his mother's home depressing and secured his own quarters. Living on the small sum allotted her by Judge Davis from her husband's estate, Mary Todd had to pay back ten thousand dollars in outstanding debts on purchases she had made while she was still the First Lady. She soon discovered that she could not afford any luxuries, that she could no longer afford to employ Elizabeth Keckley, and that she would have to move to a less expensive hotel. Mary Todd began to fear poverty.

Though Lincoln's estate amounted to approximately eighty-five thousand dollars, a sizable sum in the 1860s, Mary Todd was not told about it right away. Instead, her oldest son, Robert, and Lincoln's executor, Judge David Davis, kept her in the dark. They were probably reluctant to inform her about the money because they thought she would live too extravagantly. As a result, Mary Todd had to live off the small annual sum allotted to her by Judge Davis.

Mary Todd worried that she would be unable to pay her debts and still have enough money left for herself and her sons. To support herself, she tried to sell some of her finest dresses, which she no longer allowed herself to wear. Some enterprising merchants had approached her with an idea for raising funds. They told Mary Todd to write to wealthy Republicans for whom her husband had done favors, telling them that she was reduced to selling her clothing to raise money and asking them for a donation to spare her the embarrassment of a clothing sale. The merchants then offered to help raise the money by telling the recipients of the letters that unless they made a donation, news of Mary Todd Lincoln's poverty would be made public, to the great embarrassment of the Republican party. Mary Todd wrote to those who had bribed her to work favors for them, and to those who had benefited because of her husband's presidency. This scheme backfired when few made donations and her letters were published in the newspapers. Democrats accused Republicans of having made bribes, and angry Republicans again criticized Mary Todd Lincoln as an insensible spendthrift. Some papers even accused her of insanity. The bad publicity hurt Mary Todd's feelings terribly. In a letter to Elizabeth Keckley, she wrote, the "Republican papers are tearing me to pieces. . . . If I had committed murder in every city in this *blessed Union,* I could not be more traduced."[4]

Mary Todd's son Robert wanted to prevent his mother from creating such scenes. Embarrassed by her behavior, Robert revealed his feelings toward his mother in a letter to his fiancée,

> The simple truth, which I cannot tell to anyone not personally interested, is that my mother is on one subject [money] not mentally responsible. . . . I have no doubt that a great many people . . . wonder why I do not take charge of her affairs and keep them straight but it is very hard to deal with one who is sane on all subjects but one. You could hardly believe it possible, but my mother protests to me that she is in actual want and nothing I can do or say will convince her to the contrary.[5]

If Judge Davis, the executor of Lincoln's estate, had not dragged his feet in delivering her inheritance, Mary Todd may not have grown so paranoid about her financial circumstances. She was the last to know what

Judge David Davis, who settled Abraham Lincoln's financial affairs after his death, was secretive with Mary Todd Lincoln and was slow to give her the inheritance her husband had left for her.

sum she had coming to her, and because she felt she faced an uncertain financial future, she devoted herself to raising money. She lobbied Congress for a widow's pension fund and for the remainder of the salary owed to her husband at the time of his death. Her insistent letters appealed for money to support "the wife and sons of the man who served his country so well and lost his life in consequence."[6] Congress granted her some of this money, but, more aware of Mary Todd Lincoln's inheritance than she herself was, they did not feel the need to give her much more. Mary Todd Lincoln's reputation for extravagant spending while in the White House did not bolster much support for her financial assistance now.

By law, Mary Todd Lincoln was entitled to one third of her husband's eighty-five-thousand-dollar estate. If Abraham Lincoln had prepared a will before his death, she would likely have inherited the entire eighty-five thousand dollars. However, if a husband left no will, his wife was only eligible to receive one third of his estate, with the remainder going to the children. Judge Davis did not like Mary Todd Lincoln, and along with Robert Lincoln, he doubted that she was capable of handling the money responsibly. So Davis waited to deliver the money that was rightfully Mary Todd Lincoln's, leaving her unaware of whether or not she had enough money to maintain her own home.

To make matters worse for the grieving Mary
Todd Lincoln, in 1866, William H. Herndon,
Lincoln's former law partner in Springfield, began
lecturing around the country about Abraham
Lincoln. Herndon, who eventually wrote a biography of Lincoln that has since been widely
discredited, told sensational stories about the
Lincolns that focused on how unsuited Mary Todd
and Abraham Lincoln were for each other. Herndon
claimed that Mary Todd Lincoln's personality was a
terrible cross for Abraham Lincoln to bear. Herndon
also claimed that Lincoln had not loved Mary Todd
but instead had pined after another woman named
Ann Rutledge. Herndon implied that Mary Todd
may have been the woman Lincoln ended up with,
but that she was not his first choice. Herndon's stories and his slanderous
national lecture tour,
which earned him
money and fame, made
Mary Todd sick.[7] No

*William Herndon, Lincoln's former
law partner, became Mary Todd
Lincoln's worst enemy. He spread many
rumors and published unflattering
stories about her after Abraham
Lincoln's death.*

Herndon's Accusations

Abraham Lincoln's former law partner, William Herndon, never got along with Mary Todd Lincoln. After Abraham Lincoln's death, Herndon began lecturing around the country about Lincoln and his life. His lectures were filled with sensational claims, and he became a popular speaker. Among other things, Herndon claimed that Lincoln had never loved Mary Todd and that he had been in love with another woman. Herndon also claimed that Mary Todd Lincoln had confided in him that Lincoln was not a Christian. Angered by Herndon's accusations, Mary Todd Lincoln tried to dispel these stories, but she was unable to stop Herndon. "What more can I say in answer to this man," Mary Todd wrote, "who when my heart was broken with anguish, issued falsehoods against me & mine, which were enough to make the Heavens blush?"[8]

matter how untrue Mary Todd Lincoln felt these stories were, there was little she could do. Since her terms as First Lady, she had learned to deal with attacks on her character. Now she had to suffer through attacks on her late husband's character and on their relationship.

Health Problems

In the years following Lincoln's death, Mary Todd began to suffer more frequently from what different doctors called "nervous" symptoms. She had fevers, chills, back pain, headaches, and bladder problems. She occasionally suffered from insomnia. To fall asleep, she sometimes took the drug chloral hydrate, which in large doses could cause hysteria. Nineteenth-century doctors believed Mary Todd's problems were the result of extreme nervousness and poor mental health. In fact, Mary Todd had suffered from chronic urinary tract infections ever since Tad's birth, which had damaged her bladder. Her symptoms were probably the result of these untreated infections. Doctors, however, prescribed fresh air and travel for Mary Todd Lincoln, believing this would make her feel better. In the summer of 1867, Mary Todd and Tad traveled to a health spa in Racine, Wisconsin, where long daily walks did improve her health.

In the fall of 1867, Judge Davis finally settled Lincoln's estate. Mary Todd, Robert, and Tad Lincoln each received thirty-six thousand dollars. Mary Todd's relief at finally receiving the money due to her was soon interrupted when her friend Elizabeth Keckley published a book called *Behind the Scenes: Thirty Years a Slave, and Four Years in the White House*. Keckley claimed that she intended the book to increase public understanding for Mary

Todd Lincoln, but Mary Todd felt otherwise. She considered the book, which included personal letters she had written to Keckley, a breach of trust and friendship, and she broke off relations with Keckley completely. Once again, Mary Todd Lincoln lost a close friend.

Humiliated and feeling very alone, Mary Todd decided to go to Europe with fifteen-year-old Tad in the hopes of improving her spirits and health. In 1868, the two sailed across the Atlantic and visited Austria, France, England, Belgium, Germany, and Scotland. Mary Todd enrolled Tad in a foreign school.

Meanwhile, from abroad, Mary Todd continued to lobby Congress for money "befitting a widow of the chief magistrate of a great nation," and many statesmen grew annoyed with her behavior. As biographer Jean H. Baker wrote, Mary Todd Lincoln "cried too long and too hard" until no one wanted to listen anymore.[9] In 1870, after Mary Todd and her remaining friends had written many letters on her behalf, Congress finally voted to give Mary Todd Lincoln a three-thousand-dollar yearly widow's pension. This triumph was short-lived however, because it was soon followed by another tragedy.

Death of Another Child

In 1871, Tad became ill with pleurisy, an infection that causes water to build around the lungs. Mary

Todd brought him back to the United States, and in July 1871, Tad died at age eighteen.

Mary Todd went into a steep decline. She blamed herself for Tad's death. All the successes in her life had been followed by tragedies, and she blamed herself for not preventing them. Lincoln's election to Congress had been followed by Eddy's death. Her first successful state dinner had been followed by Willie's death. Lincoln's re-election to the presidency had been followed by his death. And now, her success with the pension bill had been followed by Tad's death. "As grievous as other bereavements have been," Mary Todd wrote to a friend shortly after the funeral, "not one great sorrow, ever approached the agony of this."[10] Robert Lincoln was also worn down by Tad's death, and his frayed nerves caused him to seek refuge in the Rocky Mountains. Mary Todd summoned her spiritualist friends and begged them to come see her. Unable to sleep, Mary Todd began taking large doses of chloral hydrate, which may have caused her to become hysterical.

Mary Todd lived with Robert Lincoln and his wife in Chicago after Tad's death. But the Great Chicago Fire, which raged through the city in the fall of 1871, uprooted her. Terrified of fire, she was afraid to use gas for lighting or cooking and moved her personal belongings for fear there would be another fire in Chicago.

She began to move frequently, staying at places like the Spiritualist Center in St. Charles, Illinois. She traveled for her health to spas, but she never remained long in one place. Sometimes she pretended to be someone else, but rarely was she able to fool anyone. Anniversaries of her different tragedies plagued her, and Mary Todd Lincoln began to rely on spiritualism more and more for comfort and relief. At seances, she claimed that the faces of Tad, Eddy, Willie, and Abraham Lincoln appeared to her. She posed for the spiritualist photographer William Mumler, who produced a picture for her that showed a ghostly image of Abraham Lincoln standing behind her with his hands placed protectively on her shoulders.

Mary Todd feared that she would lose her last son, Robert, and was constantly worried that he might become ill. Hoping that financial support would help keep him healthy, she shared her portion of Tad's inheritance with him and even loaned him more money. She moved into a Chicago hotel where she could be near him.

It was at this time that Robert became aware of his mother's increasingly odd behavior. He grew concerned over her obsessions. Certainly her fear of tragedy was understandable, but her financial practices were not, at least not to Robert. Mary Todd sewed thousands of dollars' worth of bonds into her petticoats. In Chicago stores she began to make multiple purchases of the same item. She would buy not one, but ten pairs of gloves or eight pairs of curtains, despite the fact that she did not own a home.

Robert was eager to prevent his mother from becoming a public spectacle. She had recently caused a commotion by refuting William Herndon's statements. Many people thought she was eccentric, and her strange purchases at Chicago department stores supported this belief. Mary Todd Lincoln may have found comfort in her purchases, and some of her biographers believe buying was a way for her to feel better. But Mary Todd Lincoln's contemporaries did not have the benefit of this view. Some thought that she was insane. Robert thought his mother might be buying things for her spiritualist friends and worried that she was squandering her money. On some nights in the hotel, her behavior had been delusional; she had told the hotel staff that Chicago was on fire again, and she had left her rooms half-dressed. Believing that grief had affected her mind, Robert Lincoln decided to have his mother's mental health judged by doctors.

Confinement

On May 19, 1875, three men surprised Mary Todd Lincoln at her hotel. They had been sent by Robert to escort Mary Todd to the courthouse, where a jury was waiting to judge her sanity. Under much protest, Mary Todd Lincoln rode with the men to the courthouse, where seventeen witnesses, gathered by

Robert Lincoln, Mary Todd's only surviving son, believed his mother to be mentally ill. He had her committed to a mental institution.

Robert, gave examples of her insanity.

Five doctors, relying on testimony given by those who knew Mary Todd Lincoln, pronounced her incompetent, although none of them had ever examined her. Then Robert Lincoln took the stand against his mother, testifying, "I have no doubt my mother is insane. She has long been a source of great anxiety to me. She has no home and no reason to make these purchases."[11] It took the all-male jury a total of ten minutes to conclude that Mary Todd Lincoln was insane. She was sent to the Bellevue Place asylum in Batavia, Illinois, and was forced to give up the control of her money. For a little over three months, Mary Todd stayed at Bellevue, behaving like a model patient. All the while, she plotted her escape.

Mary Todd Lincoln did not believe that she was insane. Modern-day doctors who have reevaluated her case agree that she was competent and entirely capable of living on her own. Mary Todd felt that Robert's behavior was unforgivable and knew she could not use him to help her. She knew she would need a lawyer in order to get out of Bellevue, and she tried to contact one by mail. Because all her letters were censored, Mary Todd had to secretly smuggle letters out with the help of hospital staff. She managed to send letters to old friends and members of Congress, anyone she thought could help get her out of the hospital.

It was one of her spiritualist friends who finally rescued her. Myra Bradwell was a former neighbor of Mary Todd Lincoln's, and she, too, had lost three children. She and Mary Todd Lincoln first met in 1867 and had attended some spiritualist meetings together. Now Bradwell, a lawyer who was married to an Illinois judge, worked for Mary Todd Lincoln's release. The Bradwells succeeded in their public campaign to force the administrator of Bellevue to admit that Mary Todd Lincoln could function very well in a private home. Mary Todd had already written to her sister Elizabeth Edwards in Springfield and was prepared to move in with her if released. Embarrassed by the Bradwells' campaign, Robert Lincoln finally agreed to his mother's release and accompanied her to Springfield.

In Springfield, Illinois, Mary Todd Lincoln once again made her home at Elizabeth and Ninian Edwards's house. Elizabeth understood her sister's addiction to chloral hydrate and accepted her sometimes eccentric behavior. For a year, Mary Todd stayed in Springfield and fought Robert in order to recover her money. In June 1876, finally recovering her assets from Robert, Mary Todd broke off contact with her only surviving son and left for Europe once again. As she explained to her sister Elizabeth, "[M]y former friends will never cease to regard me as a lunatic. . . . I love you but I cannot stay in Springfield. I would be much less unhappy in the midst of strangers."[12] The Edwardses' grandson, Lewis Baker, who was Tad's age and who had become a friend to Mary Todd, accompanied her to New York. Along the way, they stopped in Lexington, Kentucky, and Mary Todd visited her parents' graves.

Settling in the town of Pau, in southwest France, near the Pyrenees Mountains, Mary Todd Lincoln was unable to give up her love for American politics completely. She continued to subscribe to an Illinois newspaper, through which she kept abreast of events at home. In 1879, she broke her back in a fall. A few months later, she hurt herself again falling down the stairs. By 1880, she had asked Lewis Baker to meet her in New York. Poor health and failing eyesight had forced her to return to the Edwardses' home.

In 1881, the assassination of President James Garfield left his wife a widow. When Congress

A Tragedy Avoided
When Mary Todd Lincoln returned to America from Europe on the steamer *Amerique* in 1880, the actress Sarah Bernhardt was also aboard. The two women were talking on deck one morning when a great wave washed over the deck and knocked them down. Mary Todd Lincoln was sliding quickly toward a staircase when Sarah Bernhardt grabbed her skirts and prevented her from falling. Mary Todd Lincoln remarked regretfully that it was not yet God's will for her to die. Sarah Bernhardt later said, "I had just done this unhappy woman the only service that I ought not to have done her—I had saved her from death."[13]

granted Lucretia Garfield a five-thousand-dollar yearly pension, Mary Todd Lincoln began a campaign to secure herself at least this much. Gathering friends to write letters on her behalf, Mary Todd orchestrated one more letter-writing campaign. It was a successful one. Congress agreed to increase her pension to five thousand dollars annually, and they awarded her fifteen thousand dollars in back payments. But Mary Todd never saw the money for which she had fought. On July 15, 1882, the anniversary of Tad's death—always a hard day for her—she collapsed in her bedroom at the Edwardses' house

and died soon after from a stroke. At age sixty-four, Mary Todd Lincoln finally joined her husband and three sons in death. At her funeral in Springfield, the minister pronounced, "When Abraham Lincoln died, she died. . . . So it seems to me today, that we are only looking at death placing its seal upon the lingering victim of a past calamity."[14]

RESURRECTING
MARY TODD
LINCOLN

Mary Todd Lincoln is most often remembered for her expensive redecorating of the White House while the nation was engulfed in the Civil War and for her alleged insanity. This is not a flattering recollection of the woman who, perhaps more than any other woman before her, defined what it meant to be a First Lady.

Mary Todd Lincoln was a presidential wife who relished the role. She was an active, highly public figure. Mary Todd hosted receptions, routinely made public appearances, reviewed Union troops, visited army hospitals, raised funds for freed slaves, mothered her sons, and consoled her husband through the worst parts of the Civil War. She was one of the busiest First Ladies in history.

Before Mary Todd Lincoln's time, the White House was a run-down mansion with broken furniture, mismatched china, and torn curtains. When she left it, the White House had gas lighting, spring mattresses, enough china for state dinners, fine carpeting, beautiful wallpaper, and new rosewood furniture. It resembled the executive mansion we know today. Mary Todd's redecoration of the White House raised the executive office to a new prestige, and the renovations for which she was once ridiculed have become a lasting legacy.

At a time when communication was quicker than ever before in United States history, Mary Todd Lincoln endured some of her harshest lashes from the news media. Most Americans never met Mary Todd Lincoln; they only heard about her through the press, which alternately loved and hated her. Because the papers accused Mary Todd of everything from spying to sending medicine to the Confederates, many Americans did not like her. Some of those who met her were astonished that she was nothing like what they had read in the papers. Mary Todd's treatment by the media set a precedent for future First Ladies who would have to endure their own trials with the press.

Mary Todd Lincoln was not a modest or humble woman; she was proud and she had a short temper.

Mary Todd Lincoln is still remembered as one of the most controversial First Ladies in American history.

She was not above tongue-lashing her husband when she became angry. But there is little doubt that she and Lincoln loved each other. His death ended her happiness. Mary Todd Lincoln faced numerous obstacles to her personal happiness. Her family was torn apart by the Civil War; she was maligned by the press; she endured tragedy after personal tragedy—including her husband's assassination before her eyes; she was publicly humiliated by being forced into a mental institution by her only surviving son; and at the end of her life, she slipped into obscurity. The emotional strain these tragedies must have caused was immeasurable. Mary Todd Lincoln was an incredibly resilient woman to have endured all this. Measured against the odds she faced, Mary Todd Lincoln deserves to be remembered as a strong, proud woman who used her natural talent to perform as best she could for her family and her country.

CHRONOLOGY

1818—Born in Lexington, Kentucky.

1825—Mother dies, following a difficult childbirth.

1826—Father remarries; Mary Todd does not get along with her stepmother.

1827—Begins her formal education at Shelby Female Academy in Lexington.

1832—Attends boarding school in Lexington.

1837—Travels to Springfield, Illinois, to visit her sister.

1839—Moves to Springfield to live in the Edwards home; Meets Abraham Lincoln for the first time.

1840—Begins courtship with Abraham Lincoln despite family's opposition.

1841—Breaks off her courtship with Lincoln.

1842—Reconciles with Lincoln; They are married.

1843—First son, Robert Todd Lincoln, is born.

1846—Lincolns' second son, Eddy is born; Abraham Lincoln is elected to Congress; Mary Todd moves the family to a boardinghouse in Washington, D.C.

1850—Eddy Lincoln dies; Third son, Willie Lincoln, is born.

1853—Tad Lincoln is born.

1860—Abraham Lincoln wins the 1860 presidential election; The family moves into the White House; Begins redecorating the building.

1862—Willie Lincoln dies of typhoid fever; Mary Todd begins experimenting with spiritualism; Rumors circulate that Mary Todd harbors Confederate sympathies.

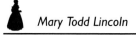

1865—Civil War ends; Abraham Lincoln is assassinated; Mary Todd Lincoln moves the family to Chicago; She begins petitioning Congress for a widow's pension.

1867—Mary Todd attempts to sell some of her clothing to raise money; Robert Lincoln begins to suspect that his mother is deranged.

1868—Elizabeth Keckley, Mary Todd's close friend and dressmaker, publishes a book about her years in the White House; Mary Todd ends their friendship; Tad and Mary Todd Lincoln travel to Europe.

1870—Mary Todd receives her widow's pension from the United States government.

1871—Tad dies of pleurisy at age eighteen.

1875—Robert Lincoln places his mother on trial for insanity; Mary Todd is declared insane by a court and is sent to Bellevue Place asylum in Illinois; Mary Todd negotiates her release and moves to her sister's home in Springfield.

1876—Mary Todd moves to Pau, France, and lives a reclusive life; She breaks off relations with her only surviving son, Robert.

1880—Ill health forces Mary Todd to return to Springfield.

1882—Mary Todd Lincoln dies in Springfield, Illinois, at age sixty-four.

CHAPTER NOTES

Chapter 1. A Controversial Woman
1. Jean H. Baker, *Mary Todd Lincoln: A Biography* (New York: W. W. Norton & Company, 1987), p. 226.
2. Paul F. Boller, Jr., *Presidential Wives* (New York: Oxford University Press, 1988), p. 124.

Chapter 2. Girlhood in Lexington, Kentucky
1. Mary Beth Norton et al., *A People and a Nation: A History of the United States*, 3rd ed. (Boston: Houghton Mifflin Company, 1990), vol. 1, p. 203.
2. Jean H. Baker, *Mary Todd Lincoln: A Biography* (New York: W. W. Norton & Company, 1987), p. 55.
3. Ibid., p. 24.
4. Ibid., p. 30.
5. Ibid., p. 61.
6. Ibid., p. 46.
7. Ibid., p. 52.
8. Ibid., p. 79.
9. Ruth Painter Randall, *Mary Lincoln: Biography of a Marriage* (Boston: Little, Brown and Company, 1953), p. 11.
10. Ibid., p. 12.
11. Baker, p. 74.

Chapter 3. The Belle of Springfield
1. Jean H. Baker, *Mary Todd Lincoln: A Biography* (New York: W. W. Norton & Company, 1987), p. 88.
2. Ibid., p. 84.
3. Ruth Painter Randall, *Mary Lincoln: Biography of a Marriage* (Boston: Little, Brown and Company, 1953), p. 19.
4. Baker, p. 85.
5. Ibid., p. 91.
6. Randall, p. 56.
7. Ibid., p. 66.
8. Baker, p. 97.
9. Randall, p. 74.
10. Baker, p. 142.
11. Ibid., p. 107.
12. Justin G. Turner and Linda Levitt Turner, *Mary Todd Lincoln: Her Life and Letters* (New York: Alfred A. Knopf, 1972), p. 46.

13. Baker, p. 120.

14. Ibid., p. 151.

Chapter 4. Mary Todd Lincoln: Political Booster

1. Jean H. Baker, *Mary Todd Lincoln: A Biography* (New York: W. W. Norton & Company, 1987), p. 126.

2. Mary Beth Norton et al., *A People and a Nation*, 3rd ed. (Boston: Houghton Mifflin Co., 1990), vol. 1, p. 390.

3. Carl Sandburg, *Abraham Lincoln* (Franklin Center, Pa.: Franklin Library, 1978), p. 192.

4. Baker, p. 162.

Chapter 5. First Lady

1. Geoffrey C. Ward, with Ric Burns and Ken Burns, *The Civil War: An Illustrated History* (New York: Alfred A. Knopf, 1990), p. 26.

2. Jean H. Baker, *Mary Todd Lincoln: A Biography* (New York: W. W. Norton & Company, 1987), p. 167.

3. Ibid., p. 181.

4. Ibid., p. 199.

5 Ibid., p. 196.

6. Ibid., p. 188.

7. Ibid., p. 197.

8. Ibid., p. 238.

9. Paul F. Boller, Jr., *Presidential Wives* (New York: Oxford University Press, 1988), p. 125.

10. Ibid., p. 231.

11. Francis Browne, *The Everyday Life of Abraham Lincoln* (Hartford: Park Publishing Co., 1886), p. 643.

12. Dorothy Kunhardt and Philip Kunhardt, Jr., *Twenty Days: A Narrative in Text and Pictures of the Assassination of Abraham Lincoln and the Twenty Days and Nights That Followed—The Nation in Mourning, the Long Trip Home to Springfield* (New York: Harper & Row, 1965), p. 4.

13. Ibid., p. 11.

Chapter 6. Widowhood

1. Jean H. Baker, *Mary Todd Lincoln: A Biography* (New York: W. W. Norton & Company, 1987), p. 247.

2. Ruth Painter Randall, *Mary Lincoln: Biography of a Marriage* (Boston: Little, Brown & Company, 1953), p. 385.

3. Ibid., p. 384.

4. Gerry Van der Heuvel, *Crowns of Thorns and Glory: Mary Todd Lincoln and Varina Howell Davis: The Two First Ladies of the Civil War* (New York: E. P. Dutton, 1988), p. 194.

5. Ibid., p. 195.

6. Baker, p. 263.

7. Ibid., p. 269.

8. Paul F. Boller, Jr., *Presidential Wives* (New York: Oxford University Press, 1988), p. 127.

9. Baker, p. xiv.

10. Ibid., p. 309.

11. Ibid., p. 321.

12. Ibid., p. 350.

13. Van der Heuvel, p. 219.

14. Ibid., p. 221.

GLOSSARY

abolitionist—One who seeks to eliminate slavery.

beau—A boyfriend.

circuit court—A court that resides at more than one place within a judicial district.

Confederacy—The Southern states that seceded from the Union and fought it during the Civil War.

Constitutional Union party—A short-lived political party formed in 1860, dedicated to preserving the federal Union.

contrabands—Slaves who became free either by escaping or by being brought to the Union lines during the Civil War.

court—To date or engage in a romance.

Free-Soiler—A member of a political party formed to prevent the spread of slavery to new United States territories.

patronage—The practice of appointing individuals to government positions for the sake of political advantage.

popular sovereignty—Doctrine that allowed the people living in a territory to decide whether or not slavery would be permitted there.

quarantine—An isolation of individuals that is intended to stop the spread of disease.

quinine—A medicine derived from the bark of the cinchona tree and sought during the Civil War as a treatment for reducing fever and preventing malaria.

specie—Money in coin form, especially gold or silver.

spiritualism—The belief that the spirits of the dead can communicate with the living.

Whig—A member of the Whig political party, which favored manufacturing and commercial interests and was succeeded by the Republican party in 1854.

FURTHER READING

Books

Baker, Jean H. *Mary Todd Lincoln: A Biography*. New York: W. W. Norton & Company, 1987.

Boller, Paul F., Jr. *Presidential Wives*. New York: Oxford University Press, 1988.

Judson, Karen. *Abraham Lincoln*. Springfield, N.J.: Enslow Publishers, Inc., 1998.

Kent, Zachary. *The Civil War: "A House Divided."* Hillside, N.J.: Enslow Publishers, Inc., 1994.

Neely, Mark E., Jr., and R. Gerald McMurtry. *The Insanity File: The Case of Mary Todd Lincoln*. Carbondale, Ill.: Southern Illinois University Press, 1986.

Randall, Ruth Painter. *Mary Lincoln: Biography of a Marriage*. Boston: Little, Brown and Company, 1953.

Somerlott, Robert. *The Lincoln Assassination in American History*. Springfield, N.J.: Enslow Publishers, Inc., 1998.

Truman, Margaret. *First Ladies*. New York: Random House, 1995.

Turner, Justin G., and Linda Levitt Turner. *Mary Todd Lincoln: Her Life and Letters*. New York: Alfred A. Knopf, 1972.

Van der Heuvel, Gerry. *Crowns of Thorns and Glory: Mary Todd Lincoln and Varina Howell Davis: The Two First Ladies of the Civil War*. New York: E. P. Dutton, 1988.

Ward, Geoffrey C., with Ric Burns and Ken Burns. *The Civil War: An Illustrated History*. New York: Alfred A. Knopf, 1990.

Internet Addresses

Mary Todd Lincoln Research Site. December 29, 1996. <http://members.aol.com/RVSNorton/Lincoln15.html.

National First Ladies' Library. "Lincoln, Mary Ann Todd." *First Ladies of the United States.* n.d. <http://www.firstladies.org/biographies/firstladies.aspx?biography=17>.

White House Historical Association. "Abraham Lincoln." *The Presidents of the United States.* 1994. <http://www.whitehouse.gov/history/presidents/al16.html>.

White House Historical Association. "Mary Todd Lincoln, 1818–1882." *The First Ladies of the United States.* 1994. <http://www.whitehouse.gov/history/firstladies/ml16.html>.

INDEX